BrightRED Results

Standard Grade
CHEMISTRY

David Hawley and Sandy McLeman

BrightRED
PUBLISHING

First published in 2009 by:

Bright Red Publishing Ltd
6 Stafford Street
Edinburgh
EH3 7AU

A CIP record for this book is available from the British Library

ISBN 978-1-906736-06-4

With thanks to Ken Vail Graphic Design, Cambridge (layout) and Tara Watson (copy-edit)

Cover design by Caleb Rutherford – eidetic

Illustrations by Beehive Illustration (Mark Turner) and Ken Vail Graphic Design, Cambridge.

Acknowledgements

Every effort has been made to seek all copyright holders. If any have been overlooked then Bright Red Publishing will be delighted to make the necessary arrangements.

Bright Red Publishing would like to thank the Scottish Qualifications Authority for use of Past Exam Questions. Answers do not emanate from SQA.

Contents

Introduction

Revising for the Standard Grade Chemistry course

Syllabus

The Standard Grade Chemistry course covers the following 15 topics:

1 Chemical Reactions

2 Speed of Reactions

3 Atoms and the Periodic Table

4 How Atoms Combine

5 Fuels

6 Structures and Reactions of Hydrocarbons

7 Properties of Substances

8 Acids and Alkalis

9 Reactions of Acids

10 Making Electricity

11 Metals

12 Corrosion

13 Plastics and Synthetic Fibres

14 Fertilisers

15 Carbohydrates and Related Substances

Assessment

There are two types of assessment – **external** and **internal**.

The **external assessment** consists of two separate examination papers: one designated **General level** which assesses grades 3 and 4 and the other designated **Credit level** which assesses grades 1 and 2.

Each examination lasts for 1 hour and 30 minutes and each paper is divided into two parts:

▸ **Part 1** which is worth **20 marks** is made up of grid questions

▸ **Part 2** which is worth **40 marks** contains questions which require written answers.

Of the 60 marks in each paper, **30 marks are allocated to *Knowledge and Understanding* (KU)** questions and the other **30 marks are allocated to *Problem Solving* (PS)** questions.

continued

Assessment – continued

The **KU** and **PS** elements are graded separately in each paper. If you attempt papers at both Credit and General levels, you will be given the better of the two grades achieved in the two papers for each element.

Practical Abilities (**PA**), which consist of techniques and investigations, are **assessed internally** and you will be awarded a grade in **PA** based on your performance.

Your grade for attainment in each of the elements **KU**, **PS** and **PA** will be recorded on your final Certificate together with an **overall grade**. The overall grade is worked out by taking an average of your grades in KU, PS and PA with a weighting of 2:2:1 in favour of KU and PS.

Structure and aim of this book

The aim of this book is to help you achieve success in the final exam by providing you with a concise coverage of the syllabus content and working through a selection of the most frequently occurring questions from past papers.

The book is divided into the 15 topics of the course and each topic:

▶ covers separately the learning outcomes at General and Credit levels in a manner which will not only help you learn the key ideas and concepts but will also allow you to gain a good understanding of them.

▶ contains General level and Credit level questions taken or adapted from past papers and provides detailed explanations and guidance in answering these questions.

▶ contains *Look out for!* sections where key aspects of the course, with which students regularly struggle, are flagged up and fully explained.

It is important that you use this book to reinforce your class learning throughout the duration of the course and not just as a revision guide in the lead up to the exams.

Good luck, and enjoy!

Chemical reactions

What you should know at General **level...**

In a **chemical reaction:**

▶ substances react together and are changed into **new substances**, i.e. different substances.
▶ the substances that react together are called **reactants** and the substances that are formed are called **products**.
▶ one or more new substance is **always** formed.

There are lots of chemical reactions which occur in our daily lives. Examples of these **everyday chemical reactions** include:

▶ hair growing on our heads
▶ iron rusting
▶ weathering of limestone buildings
▶ petrol burning in a car engine
▶ milk turning sour
▶ baking a cake.

The **signs of a chemical reaction** taking place are:

▶ **bubbles of gas** being produced.

▶ there is **an energy change**, for example heat energy can be given out causing a rise in temperature as shown opposite. Other forms of energy can be produced such as light energy, sound energy and electrical energy.

▶ there is **a colour change** as in the example opposite where **green** copper carbonate is heated and changes into a **black** coloured compound.

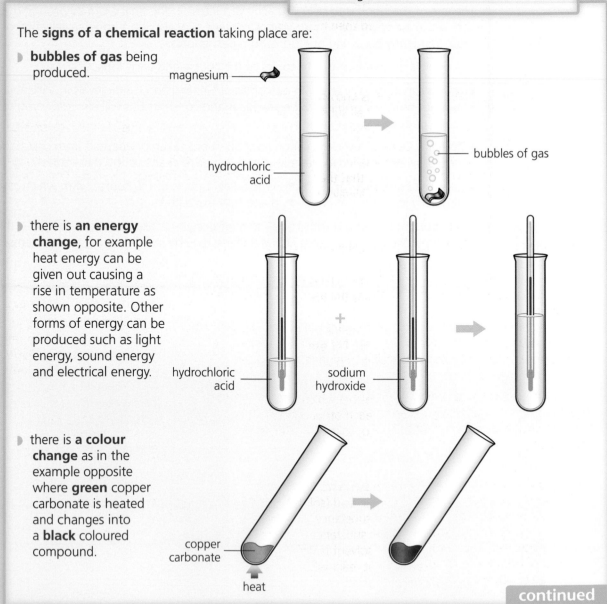

magnesium

hydrochloric acid

bubbles of gas

hydrochloric acid

sodium hydroxide

copper carbonate

heat

continued

What you should know at General level – continued

▶ **a solid is formed in a clear solution**. In the example shown below, the two **clear** and colourless solutions form a **cloudy** yellow solution. When a solution turns cloudy, it means that a solid has formed. In this example there is also another sign of a chemical reaction – a colour change from colourless to yellow.

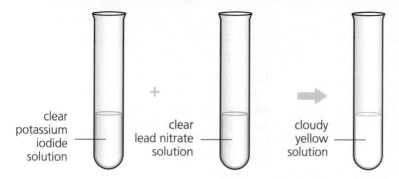

clear potassium iodide solution

clear lead nitrate solution

cloudy yellow solution

If **one** or **more** of the above is observed then a chemical reaction **must** have taken place.

Elements:
▶ are the simplest substances known and there are about 100 of them.
▶ are the building blocks for all substances in the world.
▶ are listed in a chart called the **Periodic Table**, a copy of which can be found on page 8 of the data booklet.
▶ each have a **name** and a **symbol**. For example, the symbol for the element lithium is Li and for potassium is K. Notice that the **first letter** of a symbol is always a **capital letter** and the **second**, if there is one, is always a **small letter**.

A **compound**:
▶ is a substance in which two or more elements are chemically joined together.
▶ with a name ending in '**ide**' usually contains only two elements. For example, sodium chloride contains the elements sodium and chlorine.
▶ with a name ending in '**ate**' or '**ite**' contains more than two elements – the extra element is **always oxygen**. For example, sodium chlorate contains the elements sodium, chlorine **and** oxygen.

A **mixture** contains two or more substances which are just mixed together and **not** chemically joined to each other. Vinegar, for example, is a mixture. It contains an acid, called ethanoic acid, and water.

A **solution** is:
▶ formed when a **solute** dissolves in a **solvent**. For example, vinegar is a solution in which ethanoic acid (solute) is dissolved in water (solvent). The **solute** is the substance which dissolves in the solvent and the **solvent** is the substance in which the solute dissolves. The most common solvent is water.
▶ a mixture because the solute does not react with the solvent – they are simply mixed together.

Look out for

The words 'clear' and 'colourless' are commonly used to mean the same thing but they are quite different. 'Clear' means transparent, i.e. you can see through it, whereas 'colourless' means without colour. For example copper sulphate solution can be described as a clear blue solution – 'clear' because it is transparent and 'blue' because of its colour.

Look out for

Remember that compounds with a name ending in 'ide' usually contain only two elements but there are exceptions. For example, the compound sodium hydroxide contains three elements and we can easily work out from its name that they are sodium, hydrogen and oxygen.

General question 1

Chemical reactions make new substances.

A	B	C
ice melting	food rotting	iron rusting
D	E	F
breaking glass	coal burning	finger nails growing

Identify the **two** changes which are **not** examples of chemical reactions.

Ⓐ	B	C
Ⓓ	E	F

As it states in the question **new** *substances are formed when a chemical reaction takes place. Ice is water in the solid state and when it melts it changes into water in the liquid state. Since it is still water no chemical reaction has taken place. When glass is broken it shatters into tiny little bits but these bits are still made of glass which means no new substance has been formed.*

General question 2

A student made the following statements about chemical reactions.

A	A solid is always formed.
B	A gas is always produced.
C	There is always a colour change.
D	A new substance is always formed.

Identify the statement which is true for all chemical reactions.

A	B
C	Ⓓ

The statements A, B and C are all **signs** *of a chemical reaction but none of them* **always** *happens when a chemical reaction takes place. The only thing that* **always** *happens in a chemical reaction is that a new substance is formed.*

General question 3

The grid contains the names of some metals.

A	B	C
potassium	gold	magnesium
D	E	F
copper	zinc	calcium

Identify the metal which has the symbol, K.
You may wish to use page 8 of the data booklet to help you.

Ⓐ	B	C
D	E	F

When you look at page 8 of the data booklet you find a Periodic Table with the names and symbols of the elements listed. It is a matter of taking each metal in the grid and finding it and its symbol in the Periodic Table. Potassium is the metal with symbol K.

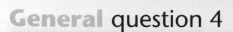

General question 4

There are many compounds of potassium.

A	potassium sulphide	B	potassium chloride	C	potassium oxide
D	potassium sulphite	E	potassium nitride	F	potassium iodide

Identify the **two** compounds which contain oxygen.

A	B	Ⓒ
Ⓓ	E	F

If a compound has a name ending in 'ate' or 'ite' then it will contain oxygen. Only one of these compounds has a name ending in 'ite' so potassium sulphite must be a correct answer. All the other compounds have names ending in 'ide' which means they contain only two elements. In potassium oxide however, oxygen is present as one of these elements.

General question 5

Lemonade can be made by dissolving sugar, lemon juice and carbon dioxide in water.

A	Sugar
B	Lemon juice
C	Carbon dioxide
D	Water

Identify the solvent used to make lemonade.

The answer is **D**.

This question is fairly straightforward provided you remember that in making a solution the solvent is the substance in which the solute is dissolved. The solutes, sugar, lemon juice and carbon dioxide have been dissolved in water to make the solution, lemonade. So water is the solvent.

General question 6

On Andy's first day in chemistry, his teacher demonstrated an experiment to the class.
Here is the report that Andy wrote in his note book.

You may have thought that the copper shrivelling up was a relevant piece of evidence but this is not one of the signs of a chemical reaction and should not be included in the answer.

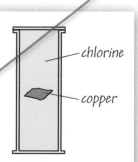

Mr Murray took this really thin brown copper and put it in a jar of greenish gas. The gas was chlorine and Mr Murray said we had to keep clear of the chorine. When the copper went in the gas it shrivelled up and then went on fire. When it stopped there was a green solid in the Jar. This is a CHEMICAL REACTION.

chlorine

copper

(a) From Andy's report, give **two** pieces of evidence which suggest that a chemical reaction has taken place.
You can see from Andy's report that there was

1)   _a colour change – the brown copper changed to a green solid,_

2)   _and there was an energy change – the copper went on fire._

(b) Give the chemical name of the green solid that is formed.

The copper has reacted with the chlorine and so the name of the
green solid formed is copper chloride.

Look out for

When stating a colour change, remember to give the colour at the start as well as the colour at the end.

Notice that the ending is 'ide' since there are only two elements in the compound.

General question 7

Name the elements present in lead nitrate.

The elements present are lead, nitrogen and oxygen.

The first of these is easy to identify – it is lead. The 'nitr' in the name indicates nitrogen and the 'ate' ending tells us there is oxygen as well.

General question 8

Air is a mixture containing nitrogen, oxygen, argon, carbon dioxide and water vapour.

(a) Why is air described as a mixture and not a compound?

This is because the substances in air are just mixed together and
not chemically joined with each other.

(b) Complete the following table using the substances present in air.

Elements	Compounds

Elements	Compounds
nitrogen	carbon dioxide
oxygen	water vapour
argon	

If the name of a substance appears in the Periodic Table then it must be an element. If not, it is a compound. Using this information, you should arrive at these answers.

Speed of reactions

What you should know at **General** **level...**

The **speed or rate of a chemical reaction** is a measure of how fast it takes place.

Different reactions have **different speeds**. For example, the reaction between hydrogen and oxygen is so fast that it results in an explosion, whereas the rusting of iron is relatively slow.

The speed of a chemical reaction is affected by **changes** in:

▶ **particle size**
Consider the reaction of magnesium ribbon and magnesium powder with dilute sulphuric acid.

You can see that the powder reacts faster with the acid than the ribbon because bubbles of gas are produced more quickly with the powder. Since the powder has a smaller particle size than the ribbon, we can conclude that **as particle size decreases, reaction speed increases**.

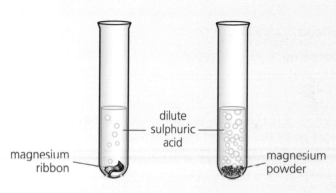

▶ **concentration**
Consider the reaction between calcium carbonate and dilute hydrochloric acid of different concentrations. The concentration of a solution can be expressed in units of moles per litre (abbreviated to mol/l). So, 0.1 mol/l hydrochloric acid is less concentrated than 1 mol/l hydrochloric acid.

It is evident that the calcium carbonate reacts more slowly with the 0.1 mol/l hydrochloric acid than it does with the 1 mol/l concentration of acid. **As the concentration of a reactant increases, reaction speed increases**.

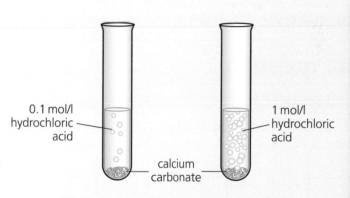

▶ **temperature**
Consider the reaction between zinc and hydrochloric acid at different temperatures.

You can see that bubbles of gas are produced more quickly at the higher temperature. This means that **as the temperature of a reaction mixture increases, reaction speed increases**.

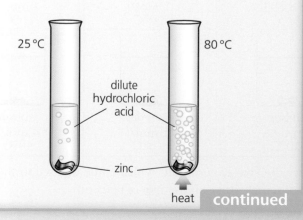

continued

What you should know at General level – continued

Everyday chemical reactions which can be affected by particle size, concentration and temperature include:

▸ Sawdust burns faster than logs because sawdust has a smaller particle size.
▸ Wounds heal more quickly in an atmosphere of pure oxygen than in air because the concentration of oxygen is greater in pure oxygen than it is in air.
▸ A car exhaust rusts at a faster speed than the bodywork because the temperature of the exhaust is higher than that of the bodywork.

A **catalyst** is a substance which:

▸ **speeds up** a chemical reaction.
▸ takes part in the reaction but by the end of the reaction is reformed.
▸ can be recovered chemically unchanged. At the end of the reaction **it is the same substance and it has the same mass as at the start of the reaction.**

Some **everyday examples of catalysts** include:

▸ **iron** used in the manufacture of ammonia.
▸ **platinum** used in manufacturing nitric acid.
▸ **nickel** used in making margarine.
▸ **transition metals** used in **catalytic converters** to speed up the conversion of harmful exhaust gases into less harmful ones.

Look out for

There is a misconception that a catalyst does not take part in a reaction because it can be recovered unchanged. A catalyst speeds up a reaction and to do this it must take part. During the reaction it does change but by the end it is reformed.

General question 1

Lesley and Scott studied the reaction of magnesium with dilute acid.

The same mass of magnesium was used in each experiment.

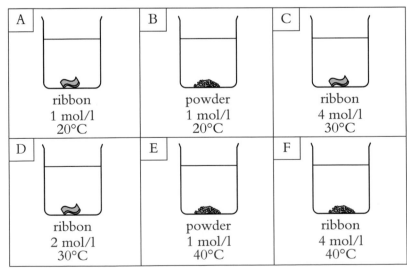

A	B	C
ribbon 1 mol/l 20°C	powder 1 mol/l 20°C	ribbon 4 mol/l 30°C

D	E	F
ribbon 2 mol/l 30°C	powder 1 mol/l 40°C	ribbon 4 mol/l 40°C

(a) Identify the **two** experiments which could be used to show the effect of temperature on the rate of reaction

Look out for

When carrying out experiments to find what effect particle size or concentration or temperature has on reaction speed, only **one** factor can be changed in order that a fair comparison can be made. For example, when investigating the effect of concentration on reaction speed, **only** the concentration of the reaction mixture is changed, other factors like particle size and temperature **must** be kept the same.

The answer is **B** and **E** since in these two experiments, the particle size of the magnesium and the concentration of the acid are the same and only the temperature of the reaction mixture is different.

(b) Identify the experiment in which the magnesium will take the longest time to react.

The magnesium will take the longest time to react in experiment **A**.

It is important to take care in this question because there is a lot of information to be processed. You are told about particle size, i.e. whether the magnesium is in ribbon or powder form and you are given the concentrations of the acid and the temperatures of the reaction mixtures. The question asks about the effect of temperature on reaction rate and so in the two experiments to be identified the temperature has to be **different** but the particle size and the concentration have to be the **same**.

If it takes the longest time then this implies you are looking for the reaction with the slowest speed. You know that the magnesium ribbon will react more slowly than the powder since it has a larger particle size. You also know that the lower the concentration and the lower the temperature the slower the reaction rate will be. Experiment A is the only one that fits these rules.

General question 2

Zinc reacts with dilute sulphuric acid.

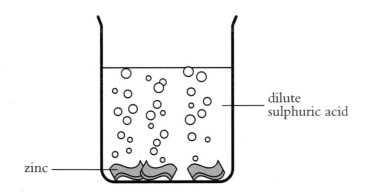

Identify the **two** factors which will speed up the reaction.

A	Using a larger volume of acid
B	Diluting the acid with water
C	Using a larger beaker
D	Heating the acid
E	Using a catalyst

The answers are **D** and **E**.

You know from learned knowledge that a reaction speeds up if the particle size is decreased, the concentration is increased, the temperature is increased or if a catalyst is used.

General question 3

The grid shows some statements of what might happen on adding a catalyst to a reaction mixture.

A	Some of the catalyst is used up.
B	The number of reactants is increased.
C	The reaction rate is increased.
D	The catalyst can be recovered unchanged.
E	The catalyst does not take part in the reaction.

Identify the **two** true statements.

The two correct statements are **C** *and* **D**.

You know that a catalyst speeds up a reaction and that it can be recovered unchanged at the end. But let's take a closer look and see why the other statements are untrue. You can eliminate A because the same mass of catalyst will be present at the end of the reaction as was present at the start. B can be eliminated because a catalyst is not a reactant – it is there at the start of the reaction and at the end. E can also be eliminated because if a catalyst is to speed up a reaction then it has to take some part in the reaction. It changes during the reaction but is reformed by the end of the reaction.

General question 4

When Stephanie added manganese dioxide to hydrogen peroxide solution, oxygen was produced.

Manganese dioxide is a catalyst.

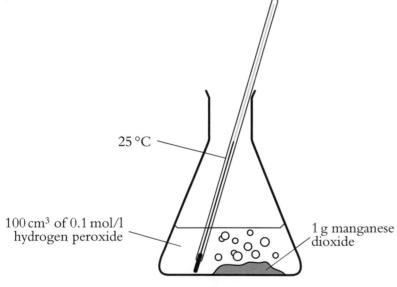

25 °C

100 cm³ of 0.1 mol/l hydrogen peroxide

1 g manganese dioxide

(a) What is the purpose of a catalyst?

A catalyst is used to speed up a reaction.

(b) What will be the mass of the manganese dioxide at the end of the reaction?

The mass of the manganese dioxide will be **1 g**.

You know that a catalyst is recovered unchanged at the end of the reaction, therefore the mass will be the same at the end as at the start.

(c) Stephanie wanted to see if raising the temperature to 35 °C would speed up the reaction.

Complete the labelling of the diagram to show how she would make her second experiment a fair test.

For the experiment to be fair, only the temperature can be different. The other factors must be exactly the same as they were in the first experiment.

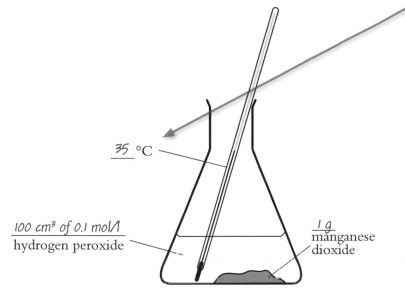

<u>35</u> °C

<u>100 cm³ of 0.1 mol/l</u>
hydrogen peroxide

<u>1 g</u>
manganese
dioxide

General question 5

Sam added magnesium to hydrochloric acid and measured the volume of hydrogen produced.

Her results for two experiments at different temperatures are shown below.

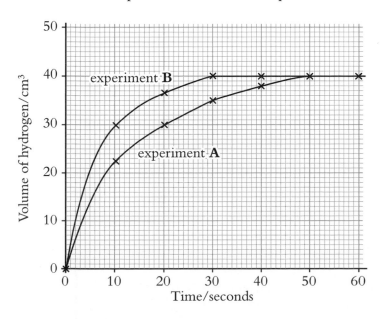

(a) What volume of hydrogen was collected in experiment **A**?

The volume of hydrogen collected in experiment **A** was **40 cm³**.

You can see from the graph for experiment A that the volume of gas levels off at 50 s. This tells us the reaction has come to an end.

(b) The same mass of magnesium and the same volume and concentration of hydrochloric acid was used in both experiments **A** and **B**.

How can you tell this from the graph?

We know this because the same volume of gas is produced in both experiments, 40 cm³.

(c) Explain which experiment was carried out at the higher temperature.

Experiment **B** was carried out at the higher temperature as the slope is steeper indicating a faster reaction rate.

*You know that the higher the temperature the faster the reaction and so you need to compare the slopes for experiments **A** and **B**. The steeper the slope the faster the reaction. The question asks you to explain so make sure you include your reasoning to gain full marks.*

Look out for

The reason why reaction speed increases as particle size decreases is due to the fact that the smaller the particle size, the larger is the surface area of the particles.

It can be quite difficult however to get to grips with the relationship between particle size and surface area.

Consider a cube with a side length of 3 cm.

Each face has an area of 9 cm² (3 × 3) and since there are 6 faces the total surface area of the cube will be 54 cm².

Now split this cube into 27 little cubes.

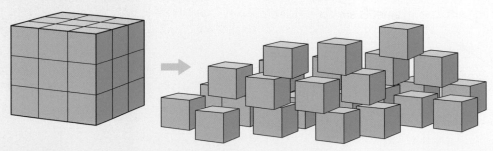

Each of the little cubes has a side length of 1 cm and each face has an area of 1 cm². Each little cube will have a surface area of 6 cm² and since there are 27 of them, their total surface area will be 162 cm².

So for the same mass of reactant, the surface area increases as the particle size decreases. This means that with smaller particle size there will be a greater area of contact between the reactants and therefore a faster reaction speed.

Chapter 3

Atoms and the Periodic Table

What you should know at General **level...**

Elements can be classified as:

▷ **naturally occurring or made by scientists.** If you look at page 8 of your data booklet you'll see that all the elements made by scientists have been asterisked (*).

▷ **solid or liquid or gas**. At room temperature only bromine and mercury are liquids, hydrogen, nitrogen, oxygen, fluorine, chlorine and the Group 0 elements are gases and the rest are solids.

▷ **metals or non-metals**. On the Periodic Tables on pages 1 and 8 there is a solid black line dividing the elements into metals and non-metals. The metals are to the left of the line and the non-metals are to the right. Be careful with hydrogen – it is a non-metal element.

Atoms are the tiny particles that are present in all elements. An **atom**:

▷ has a **nucleus** at its centre which is **positively charged.**

▷ has negatively charged **electrons** moving around outside the nucleus. The **electron arrangement** in an atom of each element is shown on page 1 of the data booklet.

▷ is **neutral** because the positive charge of the nucleus is equal to the total negative charge of the electrons.

▷ of one element is different from an atom of any other element – they vary in size and mass.

Each element in the Periodic Table has its own **atomic number**. For example if you look at page 1 of the data booklet you'll see that the atomic number of magnesium is 12 and that of iodine is 53.

The elements in the Periodic Table are arranged:

▷ in order of increasing atomic number.

▷ in vertical columns which we call **groups**. You need to know that the elements in

Group 1 are called the **alkali metals,** the elements in **Group 7** are called the **halogens** and the **Group 0** elements are called the **noble gases**.

If you look at the Periodic Table on page 8 of the data booklet you'll see that the elements which lie between Groups 2 and 3 are known as the **transition metals**.

Elements in the same group of the Periodic Table have **similar chemical properties** and the reason for this is that they have the **same number of outer electrons**. For example oxygen and sulphur have similar chemical properties since they are both in Group 6 and if you look at their electron arrangements they both have 6 outer electrons.

The **noble gases** have similar chemical properties as well but they are a family of **very unreactive elements**.

Look out for

The names of these groups, or families of elements, are often forgotten. Learning these will allow you to gain easy marks in the exam.

General question 1

The grid contains the names of some elements.

A neon	B lithium	C chlorine
D oxygen	E copper	F argon

(a) Identify the alkali metal.

A	(B)	C
D	E	F

From memory you know that the alkali metals are in Group I of the Periodic Table and if you look up page I of the data booklet you will see that lithium is in Group I.

(b) Identify the element with the highest melting point.

You may wish to use page 3 of the data booklet to help you.

A	B	C
D	(E)	F

This is a matter of finding the melting point of each element from page 3 of the data booklet. It would be a good idea to write these melting points on the grid as you find each one. It's also important that you make sure that it is the melting points you record and not the boiling points because these are also on page 3 and it is easy to confuse them. When you do this you will see that copper has the highest melting point.

(c) Identify the element which contains the lightest atoms.

You may wish to use page 5 of the data booklet to help you.

A	(B)	C
D	E	F

To answer this question you need to know the relative atomic masses of the elements and you will find them on page 5 of the data booklet. You can approach this question like the last one, by writing the relative atomic mass of each element on the grid. Don't be put off by the fact that B is also the answer to part (a) – there is no rule to say that the answers to each part of a grid question have to be different.

General question 2

An atom can be represented by a simple diagram.

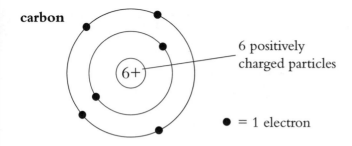

carbon

6+

6 positively
charged particles

● = 1 electron

(a) Name the structure at the centre of an atom where the positively charged particles are found.

The answer is the nucleus.

You either know this answer or you don't – there is no way of working it out from the information given.

(b) (i) Complete the diagram below to show the structure of a neon atom. You may wish to use page 1 of the data booklet to help you.

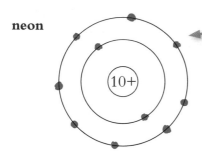

neon

What you have to do here is to enter the electrons into the shells. On page 1 of the data booklet you will see that neon has an electron arrangement of 2, 8. So you have to enter 10 electrons – 2 in the inner shell and 8 in the outer shell.

This is an example of a recall question where the learning of facts translates into marks.

(ii) Neon is found in Group 0 of the Periodic Table. Name the family of elements to which neon belongs.

Neon belongs to the noble gases.

Look out for

The number of electrons in an atom is often confused with the number of outer electrons in an atom. Take for example a sulphur atom, if you look at page 1 of the data booklet you will see that it has an electron arrangement of 2, 8, 6. This tells you that there are 2 electrons in the first shell, 8 electrons in the second shell and 6 electrons in the third and outer shell. So this sulphur atom has a total of 16 electrons (2 + 8 + 6) but only 6 of them are in the outer shell.

It is also worth remembering that with the exception of Group 0, the number of outer electrons in an atom is the same as the group number.

What you should know at **Credit** **level...**

Protons, neutrons and electrons are the small particles that make up atoms. Their relative masses, charges and positions in the atom are summarised below.

Particle	Relative mass	Charge	Position in atom
proton	1	+1	in the nucleus
neutron	1	0	in the nucleus
electron	approximately zero	−1	outside the nucleus

An atom is **neutral** and since the only charged particles present in an atom are protons and electrons, then **the number of protons must equal the number of electrons**.

Electrons in an atom are arranged in energy levels or shells which surround the nucleus. You will recall that the electron arrangements of atoms can be found on page 1 of the data booklet.

Each element has its own **atomic number** which is defined as the **number of protons** in an atom of that element. For example oxygen has an atomic number of 8 which means that any oxygen atom will contain 8 protons.

continued

What you should know at Credit level – continued

An atom has a **mass number** which is defined as **the number of protons plus the number of neutrons**.

The **number of neutrons** in an atom can be found by **subtracting its atomic number from its mass number**. Consider for example an atom of chlorine with a mass number of 35. By looking up page 1 of the data booklet you will find that chlorine has an atomic number of 17.

For this chlorine atom:

number of protons + number of neutrons = 35
number of protons = 17
This means that the number of neutrons = 18

Symbols for atoms and ions can be written showing their atomic numbers and mass numbers. Ions are charged particles that are formed when atoms lose or gain electrons. You'll find out more about ions on pages 48 and 51.

Consider as an example the following phosphide ion:

mass number → 31 $\mathbf{P}$ 3– ← charge
atomic number → 15

Given symbols like this you must be able to work out the numbers of protons, neutrons and electrons in the atom or ion.

This phosphide ion will contain **15 protons** since its atomic number is 15. By subtracting the atomic number from the mass number, you find that it contain **16 neutrons**. An **atom** of phosphorus would contain 15 electrons but since the charge on the ion is 3–, the phosphorus atom must have gained three electrons (each electron has a charge of 1–) when it formed the ion. This means the phosphide ion must contain **18 electrons**.

Atoms of the same element can have different mass numbers. These atoms are known as **isotopes**. Isotopes can be described as:

▶ atoms with the **same atomic number** but **different mass numbers,** or
▶ atoms with the **same number of protons** but **different numbers of neutrons**.

Most elements exist as a mixture of isotopes. Take chlorine for example. It has two isotopes, one known as chlorine-35 and the other as chlorine-37. Their symbols are $^{35}_{17}Cl$ and $^{37}_{17}Cl$. They both contain 17 protons but chlorine-35 contains 18 neutrons while chlorine-37 contains 20. It is important to appreciate that both isotopes of chlorine have the same chemical properties. This is because they have the same number of outer electrons.

Look out for

It is the atomic number that defines an element. This means that it is the number of protons and **not** the number of electrons that allows us to identify the element. Only in an atom will the number of electrons be the same as the number of protons. In an ion these numbers will be different.

Suppose we had a particle which contained 10 electrons. If this particle was an atom then it would contain 10 protons and have an atomic number of 10. It would be an atom of neon. However if the particle was an ion we would need to know the charge on the ion in order to identify the element. Suppose the charge was 3–. This means that 3 electrons have been gained by an atom to form this ion. The original atom must have had 7 electrons (10 – 3). This implies that it contains 7 protons and has an atomic number of 7. It is therefore an ion of the element nitrogen (N^{3-}).

Look out for

To work out the number of neutrons in an atom you subtract the atomic number from the mass number.

The **relative atomic mass of an element** is:

▶ the average mass of an atom of the element. Each element has its own relative atomic mass and some of these can be found on page 4 of the data booklet.
▶ **rarely a whole number**. This is because it is the average mass of all the atoms in the sample including the isotopes and not the mass of one particular atom.

Credit question 1

The grid contains information about the particles found in atoms.

A charge = zero	B relative mass almost zero	C charge = 1−
D found inside the nucleus	E charge = 1+	F relative mass = 1

Identify the **two** terms which can be applied to electrons.

A	Ⓑ	Ⓒ
D	E	F

This question is straightforward if you've remembered the masses, charges and positions of the particles that make up an atom. An electron has a very small mass, a charge of −1 and it is found outside the nucleus.

Credit question 2

Particle	Number of		
	protons	neutrons	electrons
A	16	18	16
B	16	18	18
C	19	20	19
D	19	21	19
E	20	20	18
F	20	20	20

(a) Identify the particle which is a positive ion.

   The answer is **E**.

(b) Identify the **two** particles which are isotopes.

   The answers are **C** and **D**.

An ion is formed from an atom when the atom gains or loses electrons. If it gains electrons then the ion formed will contain more negatively charged electrons than it has positively charged protons. As a result the ion will have a negative charge. If the atom loses electrons the ion formed will have a positive charge since it will have fewer electrons than protons. The answer must be either B or E since these are the only particles which have different numbers of protons and electrons. Particle B has more electrons than protons and so must have a negative charge. Particle E has fewer electrons than protons and so must have a positive charge.

You know that isotopes contain the same number of protons but different numbers of neutrons. Particles A and B have the same number of protons (16) but they can be ruled out because they also contain the same number of neutrons (18). Particles E and F can be ruled out on the same grounds. C and D both have 19 protons but particle C has 20 neutrons while particle D has 21.

(c) Identify the **two** particles which have the same electron arrangement as an atom of argon.

The answers are B and E.

If you look at page 1 of the data booklet you can see that argon has an electron arrangement of 2, 8, 8. Atoms with the same electron arrangement must contain the same number of electrons. The electron arrangement of argon tells us that it contains 18 (2+8+8) electrons and in the grid only particles B and E have 18 electrons.

Credit question 3

There are two different types of lithium atom, ^6_3Li and ^7_3Li.

(a) (i) What name is used to describe these different types of lithium atom?

*These different types of lithium atom are known as **isotopes**.*

(ii) A natural sample of lithium has a relative atomic mass of 6.9. What is the mass number of the more abundant type of lithium atom in the sample?

The mass number of the more abundant type of lithium atom is 7.

If you notice that these atoms of lithium have different mass numbers, i.e. 6 and 7, you'll easily come up with the answer isotopes.

You'll remember that the relative atomic mass of an element is the average mass of one atom of the element including all the atoms of each isotope. The mass of a ^6_3Li atom is 6 and that of ^7_3Li atom is 7. Since the relative atomic mass is closer to 7 than it is to 6 it follows that the ^7_3Li isotope must be more abundant.

Look out for

Mass number and relative atomic mass are often confused. Using copper as an example; it has two isotopes – one with a mass number of 63 and the other with a mass number of 65. This implies that an atom of copper-63 ($^{63}_{29}Cu$) has a mass of 63 and an atom of copper-65 ($^{65}_{29}Cu$) has a mass of 65. Notice that **mass numbers** are always **whole numbers** and they are **not** listed in the data booklet.

The relative atomic mass of copper is 63.5 (see page 4 of the data booklet). It is **not** a whole number. This is because it is the **average** mass of an atom of the element and takes into account the different isotopes of copper and their relative abundances. We can imply from its relative atomic mass that the most abundant isotope of copper is ($^{63}_{29}Cu$) since its mass of 63 is closer to 63.5. Although copper has a relative atomic mass of 63.5 there are no copper atoms with a mass number of 63.5.

(b) Complete the table to show the number of each type of particle in a $^7_3Li^+$ ion.

Particle	Number
proton	3
neutron	4
electron	2

(c) The nuclear charge of a particle is the charge on its nucleus.

What is the nuclear charge of a $^7_3Li^+$ ion?

The nuclear charge of this lithium ion is 3+.

As the question states the nuclear charge is the charge on the nucleus and must **not** be confused with the overall charge on the ion. Only the protons in the nucleus have a charge and since there are three of them and each one has a charge of 1+ the answer must be 3+.

It is the atomic number that gives us the number of protons and that number is on the lower left of the symbol. This lithium ion contains **3** protons. The number of neutrons is worked out by subtracting the atomic number from the mass number, the number on the upper left of the symbol; the number of neutrons is 7 – 3 = **4**. Calculating the number of electrons takes a bit more thought. A lithium **atom** would have 3 electrons since the number of electrons in an atom must equal the number of protons. The ion has a single positive charge which implies that when the atom forms the ion one negatively charged electron is removed from the atom. This means that the ion must contain **2** electrons.

How atoms combine

What you should know at General **level...**

Atoms can be held together by **bonds**. One type of bond is the covalent bond.

Covalent bonds:

- are formed when atoms share a pair (or pairs) of electrons. They do this in order to become more stable, by getting a full outer shell of electrons like the noble gas elements.
- are usually formed between non-metal elements. The atoms of non-metals **need** electrons to get the same stable electron arrangement as a noble gas and since both atoms need electrons they have to **share** them. It is the **unpaired electrons in the outer shell of an atom that are shared** in covalent bonding.

When two (or more) atoms are joined by covalent bonds they form **molecules**.

For example when two hydrogen atoms join together they form a molecule of hydrogen.

In this diagram and those below, the dot represents electrons on one atom and a cross represents electrons on the other atom.

Each hydrogen atom only has one electron in its outer shell. By sharing these two electrons both atoms have a full, stable outer shell like helium.

You can also represent a molecule of hydrogen as: $H-H$

A single line between two atoms represents a covalent bond. The formula for hydrogen is H_2.

Oxygen has six electrons in its outer shell so needs to share two pairs of electrons.

The formula for oxygen is O_2.

This can also be shown as: $O=O$

The = represents a **double** covalent bond or **two pairs** of shared electrons.

Like hydrogen, each molecule of oxygen contains two atoms. Any **molecule which contains two atoms** is called a **diatomic molecule**. Oxygen and hydrogen form diatomic molecules.

Nitrogen has five outer electrons and needs three more to complete its outer shell. It forms the diatomic molecule $N\equiv N$ or N_2 with a **triple** bond between the two atoms.

Other elements that form diatomic molecules are the halogens – F_2, Cl_2, Br_2, I_2 and At_2.

continued

Look out for

Make sure you understand what the single, double or triple lines between atoms mean in a formula. It is the number of covalent bonds or the number of pairs of electrons which are shared.

What you should know at General level – continued

The compound hydrogen chloride also forms diatomic molecules.
Both hydrogen and chlorine need one electron to complete their outer shell:

H $\times$ Cl

This can be shown as H $-$ Cl. Hydrogen chloride is diatomic because each molecule contains two atoms, one hydrogen atom and one chlorine atom. Hydrogen bromide (HBr) and nitrogen oxide (NO) are also examples of diatomic compounds.

Nitrogen bonds to hydrogen to form ammonia NH_3.

H $\times$ N $\times$ H
H

The nitrogen atom forms a covalent bond to three hydrogen atoms. Each hydrogen atom forms a single bond to nitrogen.

You can work out how many bonds a non-metal atom will form by calculating how many electrons are needed to complete the outer shell, i.e. to get the same electron arrangement as a noble gas.

Number of electrons needed = 8 – Group number

Number of bonds formed = 8 – Group number

For example carbon is in group 4. Carbon forms 8 – 4 = 4 covalent bonds. One carbon atom joins with four hydrogen atoms to make methane CH_4.

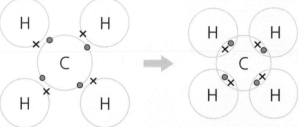

This can be shown as:

H
|
H $-$ C $-$ H
|
H

The four lines between the carbon atom and the four hydrogen atoms show that carbon forms four single covalent bonds.

Look out for

Remember it is (normally) non-metallic elements which form covalent bonds.

Look out for

You should make sure that you learn the names of the **eight** diatomic elements – hydrogen, nitrogen, oxygen and the Group 7 elements. Always write the formula with the subscript $_2$ for example H_2.

A **chemical formula** uses symbols and numbers to represent a substance. Every substance has a chemical formula. The chemical formula for methane for example is CH_4. This means there are 4 hydrogen atoms and one carbon atom in a molecule of methane.

When writing **chemical formulae for elements** you must first decide whether or not the element is made up of diatomic molecules.

▶ If it does contain diatomic molecules, then the chemical formula is written as X_2 where **X** is the symbol for the element. For example the chemical formula for **nitrogen** is N_2 and for **fluorine** is F_2.
▶ If it does not contain diatomic molecules, then the chemical formula is written as **X** where **X** is the symbol for the element. For example the chemical formula for **sulphur** is **S** and for **magnesium** is **Mg**.

continued

What you should know at General level – continued

When writing **chemical formulae for covalent compounds** you must first decide if the compound has a 'meaningful' name. You can recognise a 'meaningful' name by the presence of prefixes like mono-, di-, tri- or tetra-. (Mono means 1, di means 2, tri means 3 and tetra means 4.)

▸ If it does have a 'meaningful' name then you write the chemical formula straight from the name. For example a molecule of **di**nitrogen **mono**xide would contain 2 nitrogen atoms and 1 oxygen atom and so its chemical formula would be **N$_2$O**.

▸ If it does not have a 'meaningful' name then you must work out how many bonds each atom forms. For example in the compound carbon chloride, carbon is in Group 4 and will form 4 bonds and chlorine is in Group 7 and will form 1 bond and then you cross these numbers over:

So the chemical formula for **carbon chloride** is **CCl$_4$**.

Look out for

It is a good idea to practice writing chemical (molecular) formulae to give yourself confidence. Remember to cancel down where necessary. For example the formula of carbon sulphide is CS$_2$ (not C$_2$S$_4$) .

State symbols can be added to chemical formulae. These indicate whether the substance is in the solid, liquid or gas states. **(s)** is used for the solid state, **(l)** is used for the liquid state and **(g)** is used for the gaseous state. For example, the complete chemical formula for **hydrogen** at room temperature would be **H$_2$(g)** and that for **silicon dioxide** would be **SiO$_2$(s)**. You can use your data booklet to find the melting points and boiling points of the elements (p3) and of some compounds (p6) to allow you to insert the correct state symbol.

General question 1

The grid shows some diagrams of atoms and molecules in pure substances and mixtures.

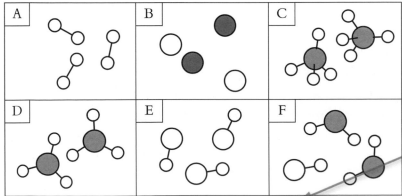

(a) Identify the compound made up of diatomic molecules.

The compound is **E**.

(b) Identify the mixture of monatomic elements.

The answer is **B**.

Here you must focus on the key words **compound** and **diatomic**. As it is a compound there has to be more than one kind of atom which rules out A, and the atoms must be joined, eliminating B. The word diatomic means only 2 atoms which rules out C, D and F.

The important words are **mixture** and **monatomic**. In a mixture the different atoms are **not** joined together. **Monatomic** means **single** atoms. There is only one box showing single atoms.

General question 2

The grid shows the formulae for some gases.

A	B	C
CH_4	CO	CO_2
D	E	F
O_2	NO_2	NH_3

(a) Identify the two gases which exist as diatomic molecules.

A	Ⓑ	C
Ⓓ	E	F

> Diatomic molecules contain two atoms. Oxygen is a diatomic element. This is shown by the subscript two in the formula for oxygen gas. Atoms in diatomic molecules do not have to be the same element. CO is also diatomic. It contains one atom of carbon and one atom of oxygen.

(b) Identify the formula for carbon dioxide.

A	B	Ⓒ
D	E	F

> Carbon dioxide is a compound with a 'meaningful' name. The **di** indicates two oxygen atoms. The formula for carbon dioxide is CO_2.

(c) Identify the molecules which contain three atoms.

A	B	Ⓒ
D	Ⓔ	F

> You already know that B and D are diatomic from part (a) so they can be eliminated. Work through **all** the other options as the question says molecules so there is more than one right answer. A has five atoms four hydrogen and one carbon. C has three atoms, two oxygen and one carbon, E has three atoms, two oxygen and one nitrogen and F has four atoms, three hydrogen and one nitrogen. Do not be put off because you have already used the letter C.

General question 3

The diagram shows a molecule of ethanoic acid.

$$H-\overset{\overset{\displaystyle H}{|}}{\underset{\underset{\displaystyle H}{|}}{C}} - C\overset{\displaystyle\diagup O}{\diagdown O-H}$$

Write the molecular formula for ethanoic acid.

The molecular formula for ethanoic acid is $C_2O_2H_4$.

> You are not meant to know the formula for ethanoic acid. You have to work it out from the information in the question. A molecule of ethanoic acid contains
>
> 2 atoms of carbon
> 2 atoms of oxygen
> 4 atoms of hydrogen
>
> This gives the chemical formula $C_2O_2H_4$ or you could write $C_2H_4O_2$. The order that you write the elements is not important but the numbers are. Make sure that you write the numbers below the line (subscript).

Look out for

Make sure you are quite clear on the meaning of the words diatomic and molecule.

What you should know at Credit **level…**

In a covalent bond the two atoms are held together by the common attraction of the two positive nuclei for the shared pair of electrons. Consider for example the covalent bond in a hydrogen fluoride molecule:

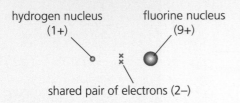

hydrogen nucleus (1+)   fluorine nucleus (9+)

shared pair of electrons (2–)

The negatively charged shared pair of electrons are attracted by both positively charged nuclei.

Diagrams showing the formula for molecules do not show the true shape of a molecule. The shape of a molecule depends on the **number of atoms** and **covalent bonds** in the molecule. Molecular models are a good way of showing the shapes of molecules. The shapes of some molecules are shown in the table below.

Compound	Formula	Shape		Description of shape
hydrogen fluoride	HF	H — F		linear
water	H_2O			bent or non-linear
ammonia	NH_3			pyramidal
methane	CH_4			tetrahedral

A dotted line shows a bond going behind the paper. The wedge shows a bond coming out of the paper.

Look out for

If you are asked to show the **shape** of a molecule do **not** draw the bonds at 90°.

Credit question 1

The grid shows the names of some elements

A	B	C
argon	chlorine	potassium

D	E	F
phosporous	sulphur	hydrogen

(a) Identify the *two* elements which form a linear molecule.

A	Ⓑ	C
D	E	Ⓕ

(b) Identify the *two* elements which would form a covalent compound with the formula of the type X_3Y_2.

A	B	C
D	Ⓔ	Ⓕ

Any molecule made from two atoms joined by a single covalent bond will be linear. Hydrogen chloride HCl is a linear molecule.

The important words here are **two** and **covalent**. Potassium is a metallic element and will not form covalent bonds. Argon is a non-metal but it is also a noble gas. You will need to work out how many bonds each of the other elements can form. Use the formula:
Number of bonds = 8 – Group Number to calculate the number of bonds. (Group numbers are shown in data booklet p8)
Cl forms 8 - 7 = 1 covalent bond
P forms 8 – 5 = 3 covalent bonds
S forms 8 – 6 = 2 covalent bonds
H forms 8 – 7 = 1 covalent bond
The formula X_3Y_2 means that X forms 2 bonds and Y forms 3 bonds. X is sulphur and Y is phosphorus. (S_3P_2)

Credit question 2

In a hydrogen molecule the atoms share electrons in a covalent bond.

(a) Explain how the covalent bond holds the two hydrogen atoms together.

<u>A covalent bond is the attraction between both positive nuclei and the shared electrons.</u>

When you are asked to explain an answer you cannot use the explanation given in the question. Just using 'share electrons' will not get you any marks.

(b) (i) Draw a diagram showing all the outer electrons to represent a molecule of ammonia, NH_3.

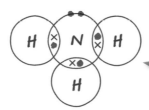

(ii) Draw another diagram to show the shape of an ammonia molecule.

Use your data booklet (p8) to find out that nitrogen has 5 electrons in its outer shell. Hydrogen only has one electron.

When you show the **shape** of molecules you must try to make some attempt to show the molecule in **three dimensions**. In the answer to (b)(i) the drawing looks as though the nitrogen–hydrogen bonds are at 90°. Any diagram showing that the bonds are **not** at ninety degrees is needed.

Look out for

You should practice drawing diagrams to show how outer electrons form a covalent bond.

Fuels

A fuel:

▹ is a substance that burns to give out heat energy. Some examples of substances used as fuels are coal, gas and wood. These are all burnt to produce heat. Any reaction which produces heat energy, is called an **exothermic** reaction.

▹ reacts with oxygen when it burns. You can use the word **combustion** as another word for burning. Usually the oxygen needed for combustion comes from the air. Air is a mixture of gases but mainly oxygen and nitrogen. The **test for oxygen** is that it relights a glowing splint. Air will allow substances to burn but will not relight a glowing splint since there is not enough oxygen in the air for that to happen.

Look out for

Remember the composition of air is approximately 80% nitrogen and 20% oxygen.

The fossil fuels:

▹ are coal, oil, and gas. These were formed millions of years ago by the effect of heat and pressure on the remains of once living organisms. In areas where these organic remains were mainly plant material **coal** was produced. Where the remains were mostly marine life, **oil** and **gas** were produced.

▹ are a **finite resource** – there is a limited supply of them. It took millions of years for fossil fuels to form but it will take a relatively short time to use them up. We depend on oil and gas for much of our energy, but as the supplies of these become limited their prices will rise. This is sometimes called the fuel crisis. Alternative sources of energy are being developed but will they be able to do the same job?

Crude oil:

▹ is a mixture of compounds – mainly **hydrocarbons**. These hydrocarbons have specific melting points and boiling points.

▹ is separated into fractions by **fractional distillation** and this separation is dependent upon the fact that the hydrocarbons have different boiling points. The oil is vapourised and passes up the fractionating column. As the vapours rise up the column they cool and turn to liquids which are run off as fractions at various points in the column.

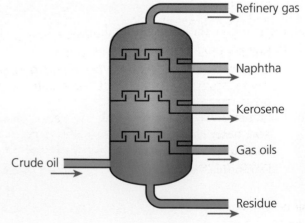

Note the names of the fractions in the diagram. Petrol forms part of the naphtha fraction, jet fuel in the kerosene fraction and diesel in the gas oil fraction.

A **fraction** is a group of compounds with similar boiling points. Different fractions have different boiling point ranges, properties and uses.

As the boiling point range of the fractions increase the:

▹ **viscosity** increases. The gas oil fraction is more viscous (less runny) than the naphtha fraction.
▹ **rate of evaporation** decreases. It takes kerosene longer to evaporate than petrol.
▹ **flammability** decreases. It is more difficult to ignite fuel oil than to ignite petrol.

continued

What you should know at General level – continued

Hydrocarbons:

▶ are compounds which contain **carbon** and **hydrogen** only. For example CH_4 is the main component of natural gas.

▶ burn in a plentiful supply of air, and undergo complete combustion to produce carbon dioxide and water. For example

$$CH_4 + 2O_2 \rightarrow CO_2 + 2H_2O$$

Limewater is used to test for carbon dioxide. It will turn cloudy if carbon dioxide is present. **Blue** cobalt chloride paper can be used to test for water. The paper will turn **pink** with water.

▶ can produce poisonous carbon monoxide gas when burnt in a limited supply of air. This is called incomplete combustion.

There are several **pollution problems** associated with the use of fossil fuels such as:

▶ **slag heaps** from coal mines. These are not pretty to look at and the material they are composed of makes it difficult for plants to grow on them.

▶ **acid rain**. Some types of coal and oil contain significant amounts of sulphur. When sulphur or sulphur compounds are burned they produce **sulphur dioxide**. This gas dissolves in rain water to make acid rain. Acid rain harms plant growth and corrodes metals. Removing these sulphur compounds before the fuel is burned reduces air pollution and acid rain.

▶ **oil spills** from tankers at sea. The spilt oil causes problems for wildlife, particularly sea birds by coating their feathers with oil.

▶ **carbon dioxide** from burning fossil fuels. There is a small amount of carbon dioxide in the air but burning fossil fuels has increased the amount. Carbon dioxide is a **greenhouse gas** and is contributing to **global warming**.

▶ **soot** from the incomplete combustion of coal. This coats buildings and makes them appear dirty.

▶ **more acid rain** caused by oxides of nitrogen. Nitrogen and oxygen from the air react together in petrol engines to produce poisonous oxides of nitrogen.

▶ **carbon monoxide** from the incomplete combustion of fuels.

▶ **lead compounds**. These were added to petrol to improve its combustion but as they are toxic they were banned from use in petrol in the UK in 2000.

Air pollution caused by burning petrol in cars can be reduced by:

▶ fitting **catalytic convertors** to car exhausts. They convert the poisonous carbon monoxide and oxides of nitrogen into less harmful gases.

▶ decreasing the fuel to air ratio. This means injecting less petrol into an engine for the same amount of air. This allows more complete combustion so there is less carbon monoxide produced.

Look out for

You should learn the tests for carbon dioxide, water and oxygen. In all tests you must give the **name** of the substance you would use and the **result**. Remember if there is a colour change as with the cobalt chloride paper you must state the colour **before** and **after** the test.

Look out for

You should know the causes of acid rain. Sulphur dioxide **and** nitrogen oxides cause acid rain.

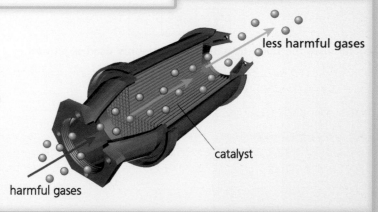

less harmful gases

catalyst

harmful gases

General question 1

The grid shows the formulae of some gases.

A	B	C
CO_2	N_2	H_2O

D	E	F
NO_2	CO	O_2

> Hydrocarbons contain carbon and hydrogen. **Any** compound of carbon will produce carbon dioxide when burned in a good supply of oxygen (or air). Also **any** compound containing hydrogen will produce water (or steam) when burned.

(a) Identify the two gases produced by the complete combustion of hydrocarbons.

Ⓐ	B	Ⓒ
D	E	F

(b) Identify the gas whose presence will be most reduced by reducing the fuel to air ratio.

A	B	C
D	Ⓔ	F

> Carbon monoxide is produced when hydrocarbons burn in a limited supply of air. When the amount of fuel is reduced there will be a better supply of air for the fuel to burn so the amount of carbon **monoxide** will be reduced.

General question 2

The grid shows the names of fractions produced from crude oil.

A	B	C
refinery gas	bitumen	kerosene

D	E	F
light gas oil	petrol	heavy gas oil

(a) Identify the most flammable fraction.

Ⓐ	B	C
D	E	F

> The most flammable fraction will contain the smallest molecules. Gases have smaller molecules than liquids.

(b) Identify the fraction which is commonly used as jet fuel.

A	B	Ⓒ
D	E	F

> This is something you need to know. You cannot work it out. It is a good idea to learn a use for each of the fractions from refining.

General question 3

Coal is a fossil fuel. Fossil fuels are a finite resource.

(a) What is meant by the term **finite**?

*There is a fixed or **limited quantity** of that substance.*

(b) There are a number of pollution problems associated with the use of coal as a fuel.
Give an example.

Acid rain.

> There are a number of ways to answer this question and still get the mark.
> If something is described as finite it means there is a fixed or **limited quantity** of that substance. Or here you could say that once it is used it **cannot be recycled or used again**.

> As there are a number of problems there are a number of answers. You are not being asked to explain so you do not need to write in sentences. Examples of pollution would include – **global warming, slag heaps, dirty buildings, acid rain** etc. You are not asked for an explanation of these so do not go into details. Do make sure you read the question carefully, it would be wrong to answer oil slicks as it specifies coal not fossil fuels.

General question 4

Crude oil is transported to refineries where it is processed.

(a) Describe how oil was formed.

Oil was formed over millions of years by the effect of heat and pressure on the remains of marine life.

> It is worth learning this definition, just remember to replace **marine** with **plant** if you are asked how coal was formed.

(b) The diagram shows one of the processes that happens in an oil refinery.

Fraction and boiling point range

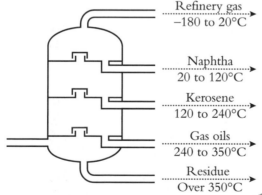

Refinery gas
−180 to 20°C

Naphtha
20 to 120°C

Kerosene
120 to 240°C

Gas oils
240 to 350°C

Residue
Over 350°C

(i) Name this process.

This process is called fractional distillation.

(ii) Which fraction is used as the main source of petrol.

*Petrol is extracted from the **naphtha** fraction.*

(iii) Some sources of crude oil contain a large number of sulphur compounds.
Why are sulphur compounds removed from the fraction which is to be used as petrol?

*Burning sulphur compounds produces sulphur dioxide, one of the causes of **acid rain**.*

> Since the word refinery appears in the question you are better to not use the term refining but use the term **fractional distillation**.

> Sulphur compounds also tend to be poisonous and can poison catalytic convertors. Either of these answers will do.

31

What you should know at Credit **level...**

At Credit level you will be expected to know the typical range of the number of carbon atoms in the hydrocarbon molecules of a fraction. The actual hydrocarbons in each fraction will vary from refinery to refinery and depend on the source of the crude oil. One set of typical fractions is listed in the table below.

Fraction name	Number of carbon atoms	examples of uses
Refinery gas	$C_1 - C_4$	propane and butane for barbeques
Naphtha	$C_5 - C_{12}$	petrol C_5-C_8
Kerosene	$C_{10} - C_{16}$	jet fuel
Gas oils	$C_{15} - C_{35}$	diesel and fuel oil for transport
Residue	$> C_{30}$	bitumen and tar for roads

The same hydrocarbon may appear in more than one fraction. Molecules of C_{11} are found in both petrol and jet fuel, C_{16} molecules can be found in both the kerosene and gas oil fractions. The uses made of each fraction depend on the properties of that fraction. As the size of the hydrocarbons increase the boiling points increase because the weak forces between the molecules increase. The increase in these weak forces also causes the increase in viscosity and the decrease in the volatility of the fraction.

When a fuel burns to produce CO_2 and H_2O the oxygen comes from the air. The **carbon** in the CO_2 has to have come from the hydrocarbon as does the **hydrogen** in the H_2O. Therefore carbon dioxide and water show the presence of carbon and hydrogen in a fuel.

Catalytic convertors contain **transition** metals. **Platinum, palladium** and **rhodium** are all used as catalysts in catalytic convertors. The pollutant gases nitrogen dioxide and carbon monoxide are changed by a catalytic convertor into less harmful nitrogen and carbon dioxide:

$$2NO_2 \rightarrow N_2 + 2O_2$$
$$2CO + O_2 \rightarrow 2CO_2$$

Reducing the quantity of fuel going to the engine also reduces the amount of carbon monoxide. By reducing the fuel to air ratio there is more complete combustion.

Look out for

You should be able to recognise fuels which are **not** hydrocarbons. For example if carbon monoxide is burned you cannot get water as a product. If hydrogen is the fuel the product is water, you cannot get oxides of carbon as the product.

Credit question 1

The grid shows the formulae of some oxides.

A		B		C	
	CO_2		CO		SO_2
D		E		F	
	NO_2		H_2O		SO_3

(a) Identify the oxide created by the high energy spark in a car engine.

A	B	C
(D)	E	F

Nitrogen is not very reactive but the high energy of the spark in a car engine will allow it to react with oxygen to produce nitrogen oxides so the answer is D.

(b) Identify the oxide which will be produced by burning a hydrocarbon but which would **not** be produced by burning carbon.

A	B	C
D	(E)	F

Burning carbon can produce both CO_2 and CO. Burning a hydrocarbon can produce CO, CO_2 and H_2O. **H_2O can not be produced by burning carbon.** Some questions can be quite confusing, take care to answer exactly what they ask.

Credit question 2

The distillation of crude oil produces a number of different fractions.

Fraction	Number of carbon atoms per molecule
A	1–4
B	4–10
C	10–16
D	16–20
E	20+

crude oil

Petrol contains a mixture of hydrocarbons with molecules containing (mainly) between 5 and 8 carbon atoms so will come from fraction B. Note that this is not an exact match because this fraction will also be the source of other products. **You should learn at least one use for each fraction**.

(a) Which fraction is used to produce petrol?

Fraction **B**.

(b) Which fraction contains the least flammable hydrocarbons.

The answer is **E**.

Flammability depends on the number of carbon atoms in a molecule. The greater the number of carbon atoms the less flammable is the hydrocarbon.

Credit question 3

Cars which use petrol as a fuel are fitted with catalytic convertors.

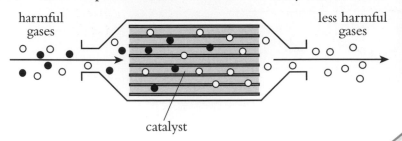

harmful gases → catalyst → less harmful gases

(a) Name a metal used as the catalyst in a catalytic convertor.

Platinum

> There are a number of different transition metals used as catalysts in convertors. You are being asked for the **name** of a metal not the **type** of metal. It is not good enough to say transition metal you will need to give a specific name. **Platinum, rhodium** or **palladium** are all currently used.

(b) Why are compounds of sulphur removed from fuels to be used in cars?

When compounds of sulphur burn they produce sulphur dioxide. Sulphur dioxide is a gas which dissolves in rain water to form acid rain.

> There are two possible answers here. Many compounds of sulphur are poisonous and will poison the catalytic convertor.

(c) Another way of reducing pollution from car engines is to reduce the fuel to air ratio.
Explain why this reduces pollution.

*In a limited supply of air hydrocarbon fuels produce carbon monoxide on combustion. With less fuel there will be more oxygen for the hydrocarbon to burn more completely so there will be **less carbon monoxide** (but more carbon dioxide) produced.*

Credit question 4

Crude oil is separated into different fractions at an oil refinery.

Fraction and boiling point range

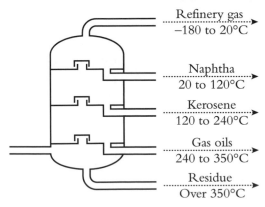

Refinery gas
−180 to 20°C

Naphtha
20 to 120°C

Kerosene
120 to 240°C

Gas oils
240 to 350°C

Residue
Over 350°C

(a) What property of the substances in crude oil is used to separate the fractions?

Different substances have different **boiling points** and separation depends on this.

(b) In which fraction will heptane be found?

You may wish to use page 6 of the data booklet.

It is in the naphtha fraction.

(c) Why is the gas oils fraction more viscous than the naphtha fraction?

The molecules in the gas oils fraction are larger than those in the naphtha fraction so it is more viscous.

(d) Which fraction will be most flammable?

The **refinery gas** fraction is the most flammable.

If a question suggests you may use the data booklet it is best to use it. You will find the boiling point of heptane is 98°C so it will be found in the **naphtha** fraction.

All molecules have weak attractions between them. Large molecules have stronger attractions between them than small molecules. These attractions are broken when the liquid flows. The more viscous a liquid is the less flowing it is. You know **gas oils are larger hydrocarbons** and have stronger attractions therefore it will be more viscous.

Small molecules are volatile and easier to ignite. Since gases are made of smaller molecules than liquids the refinery gas fraction is the answer.

Credit question 5

Methanol, $CH_3OH(l)$, and hydrogen, $H_2(g)$ have both been suggested as possible fuels for the future.

(a) Suggest an advantage and a disadvantage of using hydrogen as a fuel.

(b) Methanol produces CO_2 and H_2O when burned.

Explain why this does not show that methanol contains oxygen.

The oxygen in the CO_2 and H_2O may have come from the air when the fuel was burned.

One advantage would be that hydrogen is renewable as it can be produced from water. Another advantage would be that hydrogen does not produce CO_2 (a greenhouse gas) when burned. A disadvantage would be the volume of storage needed for the gas or the difficulty in extracting hydrogen from water. Remember you have to say which would be an advantage and which a disadvantage. Giving 'renewable and cost' only as your answer does not say which is the advantage.

Structures and Reactions of Hydrocarbons

What you should know at General **level...**

Alkanes:

▶ are hydrocarbons.
▶ are used as fuels. Methane is the gas commonly burned in central heating systems; octane is found in petrol.
▶ have names that end in **ane** and can be represented by a name, a molecular formula, a shortened structural formula or a full structural formula. These are shown in the table which lists the first eight alkanes.

You will find a set of data about the alkanes on page 6 of the data booklet. You should **learn** the **names** and the **number of carbon atoms** in each alkane but never guess. Use your data booklet to check.

Name	Molecular formula	Shortened structural formula	Full structural formula
methane	CH_4	CH_4	H | H−C−H | H
ethane	C_2H_6	CH_3CH_3	H H | | H−C−C−H | | H H
propane	C_3H_8	$CH_3CH_2CH_3$	H H H | | | H−C−C−C−H | | | H H H
butane	C_4H_{10}	$CH_3CH_2CH_2CH_3$	H H H H | | | | H−C−C−C−C−H | | | | H H H H
pentane	C_5H_{12}	$CH_3CH_2CH_2CH_2CH_3$	H H H H H | | | | | H−C−C−C−C−C−H | | | | | H H H H H
hexane	C_6H_{14}	$CH_3CH_2CH_2CH_2CH_2CH_3$	H H H H H H | | | | | | H−C−C−C−C−C−C−H | | | | | | H H H H H H
heptane	C_7H_{16}	$CH_3CH_2CH_2CH_2CH_2CH_2CH_3$	H H H H H H H | | | | | | | H−C−C−C−C−C−C−C−H | | | | | | | H H H H H H H
octane	C_8H_{18}	$CH_3CH_2CH_2CH_2CH_2CH_2CH_2CH_3$	H H H H H H H H | | | | | | | | H−C−C−C−C−C−C−C−C−H | | | | | | | | H H H H H H H H

continued

What you should know at General level – continued

If you look at the molecular formulae in the table you should see a pattern. Can you see the link between the number of carbon atoms and the number of hydrogen atoms? If you double the number of carbon atoms and add 2 you get the number of hydrogen atoms. For example in butane there are 4 carbon atoms, $(2 \times 4) + 2 = 10$ gives you the number of hydrogen atoms. If there are "n" carbon atoms there are "$2n + 2$" hydrogen atoms. This gives the **general formula** for the alkanes, C_nH_{2n+2}. You can use this to get the molecular formula of any alkane. For example if an alkane has 12 carbon atoms it will have $2 \times 12 + 2 = 26$ hydrogen atoms so the molecular formula will be $C_{12}H_{26}$.

▸ are **saturated** hydrocarbons. This means they contain **carbon to carbon** single bonds only. You can see this in the full structural formulae in the table.

Look out for

It is important to learn the names of alkanes. You can find them on page 6 of data booklet but you do not get the formulae listed there. The names are listed in order of the number of carbon atoms per molecule. Methane contains one carbon, ethane two carbons and so on. Don't guess! Most mistakes involve the names of the first four alkanes. Some pupils use a mnemonic to help them remember the names of the first four alkanes:

Mothers **e**at **p**eeled **b**ananas

methane **e**thane **p**ropane **b**utane

A common error is to confuse **propane** (3 carbon atoms per molecule) with **pentane** (5 carbon atoms per molecule). You should see that the prefix (first part of the name) used in the alkanes is related to names you will have met in maths. For example a **hex**agon has six sides. **Hex**ane contains six carbon atoms. These prefixes are also used in alkenes.

Alkenes:

▸ form another set of hydrocarbons.
▸ have names that end in **ene**. Like the alkanes they can also be represented by a name, a molecular formula, a shortened structural formula and a full structural formula as shown in the table.

Name	Molecular formula	Shortened structural formula	Full structural formula
ethene	C_2H_4	$CH_2=CH_2$	H–C=C–H with H,H below
propene	C_3H_6	$CH_3CH=CH_2$	H–C–C=C–H structure
butene	C_4H_8	$CH_3CH_2CH=CH_2$	H–C–C–C=C–H structure
pentene	C_5H_{10}	$CH_3CH_2CH_2CH=CH_2$	H–C–C–C–C=C–H structure
hexene	C_6H_{12}	$CH_3CH_2CH_2CH_2CH=CH_2$	H–C–C–C–C–C=C–H structure

continued

What you should know at General level – continued

Although these alkenes have the double bond at the end of the chain, it could be in a different position in the chain and still be an alkene. For example the hydrocarbon with the full structural formula shown alongside would still be classified as an alkene because it contains a carbon–to–carbon double bond.

The names of the first five alkenes can be found on page 6 of the data booklet.

▸ have the **general formula C_nH_{2n}**. Using this formula you can work out the molecular formula for any alkene. For example if an alkene contains 10 carbon atoms it will contain $2\times10 = 20$ hydrogen atoms. This will give the molecular formula $C_{10}H_{20}$.

▸ are **unsaturated** hydrocarbons. They contain at least one **carbon-to-carbon double bond.** Any compound which contains a carbon to carbon double bond is unsaturated. Alkenes are only one set of unsaturated compounds.

▸ rapidly **decolourise bromine solution.** This is used to test for unsaturation. Bromine solution is **decolourised** by all unsaturated compounds.

▸ take part in an **addition reaction** with bromine. In an addition reaction small molecules, usually diatomic, add **across** the double bond. For example when bromine solution is decolourised by propene the formula equation for the reaction is:

$$C_3H_6 + Br_2 \rightarrow C_3H_6Br_2$$

Using structural formula for this same reaction:

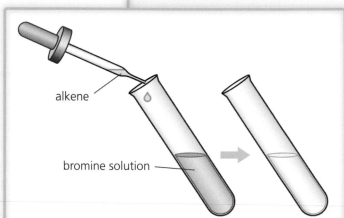

Hydrogen will also add across a double bond. For example hydrogen adds across the double bond in ethene to make ethane:

ethene + hydrogen → ethane

In an addition reaction there are **two reactants** but only **one product**.

continued

Look out for

You must use the word **decolourised** when describing this test. This is the word markers look for – do not use any other like discoloured. Remember to give the test **and** the result.

are more reactive molecules than alkanes but the supply of naturally occurring alkenes is limited. The oil industry can produce alkenes by **cracking.** The fractional distillation of crude oil tends to produce more long chain hydrocarbons than are needed. Cracking uses these long chain molecules to produce smaller more useful hydrocarbons. Some of these smaller hydrocarbons will be alkenes.

An example of a cracking reaction is:

$$C_{20}H_{42} \rightarrow C_8H_{18} + C_8H_{16} + C_4H_8$$

Notice that the total numbers of carbon and hydrogen atoms are the same on both sides of the equation.

Looking at the number of carbon atoms: 20 on the left hand side and $8 + 8 + 4 = 20$ on the right hand side and the number of hydrogen atoms: 42 on the left hand side and $18 + 16 + 8 = 42$ on the right hand side.

Equations

Equations are used throughout all topics in Chemistry. You may come across several different kinds of equations.

Word equations are used to represent a chemical reaction in words. In any equation you must write the reactants on the left hand side of the arrow and the products on the right hand side of the arrow.

reactants → products
the arrows means 'changes into'

Take for example methane which burns in oxygen to produce carbon dioxide and water.

methane + oxygen → carbon dioxide + water

If you find that you run out of space to fit the words onto one line do **not** continue as if you were writing a piece of script but use two lines as shown

methane + oxygen → carbon dioxide + water

Formula equations use symbols and formulae to represent reactants and products. At General level you do not need to be able to balance equations so do not get too worried about this. You do need to make sure that formulae are **correct**. As a formula equation, the above reaction becomes

$$CH_4 + O_2 \rightarrow CO_2 + H_2O$$

If you count the numbers of each atom you should see that there are 4 atoms of hydrogen on the reactants side but only two atoms of hydrogen on the products side. This means that the equation is **not** balanced but you should see that the formulae are all correct. Be careful that you use the correct formulae for diatomic elements like oxygen.

Look out for

Practice writing equations, you should be confident about tackling both word and formula equations.

General question 1

The grid shows the names of some hydrocarbons.

A	B	C
methane	hexane	propane
D	E	F
propene	pentene	butane

(a) Identify the hydrocarbon with **six** carbon atoms in the molecule.

A	Ⓑ	C
D	E	F

This a common type of question. Look at page 6 of the data booklet. Counting up from methane having one carbon atom you should get hexane having 6 carbon atoms. You can check the others and write the number of carbon atoms alongside the names in the question grid.

(b) Identify the two hydrocarbons which are alkenes.

A	B	C
Ⓓ	Ⓔ	F

The names of the alkenes all end in ene. The question asks for two so make sure you circle **both**.

General question 2

The grid shows the formulae for some hydrocarbons.

A	B	C
CH_4	C_2H_4	C_3H_8
D	E	F
C_7H_{16}	C_8H_{18}	C_3H_6

(a) Identify the **two** hydrocarbons which could be produced when propane(C_3H_8) is cracked.

Ⓐ	Ⓑ	C
D	E	F

Cracking produces **smaller** molecules so you need to look for molecules with **fewer** than three carbon atoms. There are only two. In cracking the total number of carbon atoms and hydrogen atoms must stay the same. You can check your answer by adding CH_4 (A) and C_2H_4 (B) which gives you three carbon atoms and eight hydrogen atoms, the same as propane. **Both** must be circled.

(b) Identify the **two** unsaturated hydrocarbons.

A	Ⓑ	C
D	E	Ⓕ

Here you are looking for alkenes as they are unsaturated. You need to know that the general formula for the alkenes is C_nH_{2n}. Using this formula you can see that there are twice as many hydrogen atoms as carbon atoms giving you B and F. **Both** must be circled.

Look out for

Make sure that you can tell the difference between alkanes and alkenes. Learn the **general formula** for both. Read the name endings carefully. You need to be able to recognise alkanes and alkenes from their names or any of the types of formulae used. Remember that alkanes are saturated and alkenes are unsaturated.

(c) Identify the hydrocarbon with the highest boiling point.

You may wish to use page 6 of the data booklet to help you

The answer is E, octane.

The larger the molecule the higher the boiling point. This should direct you to box E which is the answer. You can check page 6 but first you need to work out the names of all the hydrocarbons in the grid. You should work out that box E contains the formula for octane. The boiling point of octane is given as 126°C which you should see is the highest boiling point for the hydrocarbons listed.

General question 3

Decane, $C_{10}H_{22}$, is a compound found in the kerosene fraction obtained from crude oil.

(a) To which family of hydrocarbons does decane belong?

It is an alkane.

(b) Decane can be broken down into a mixture of saturated and unsaturated hydrocarbons.

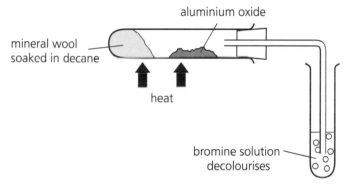

aluminium oxide

mineral wool
soaked in decane

heat

bromine solution
decolourises

Name endings give a clue to which family a hydrocarbon is in. Since decane has a name that ends in **ane** it must be an **alkane**.

(i) What is meant by a **saturated** hydrocarbon.

*A saturated hydrocarbon **contains carbon to carbon single bonds only**.*

(ii) Decane can break down in the following way:

$$C_{10}H_{22} \rightarrow C_7H_{16} + \mathbf{X}$$

Write down the molecular formula for **X**.

The formula for X is C_3H_6.

This is an example of cracking. The number of carbon atoms and hydrogen atoms on the products side must add up to the same as on the reactants side. The number of carbon atoms in X must be 10 − 7 = 3 and the number of hydrogen atoms is 22 − 16 = 6.

What you should know at **Credit** **level...**

Alkanes form a **homologous** series. That is a series of compounds, with **similar chemical properties**, for which a **general formula** can be written. All alkanes are saturated and have the **general formula** C_nH_{2n+2}. As with all homologous series there is a gradual change in **physical** properties. If you look at page 6 of the data booklet you will see that as the size of the alkane molecules increase both the melting points and boiling points increase.

Cycloalkanes are hydrocarbons with the **general formula** C_nH_{2n}. They are **saturated** hydrocarbons as they contain carbon to carbon single bonds only. You can see this in their structural formulae.

continued

What you should know at Credit level – continued

Name	Molecular formula	Structural formula
cyclopropane	C_3H_6	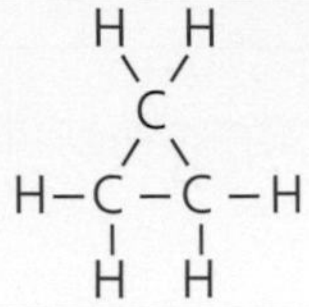
cyclobutane	C_4H_8	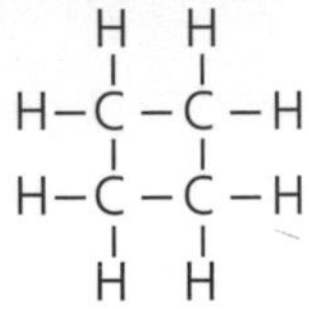
cyclopentane	C_5H_{10}	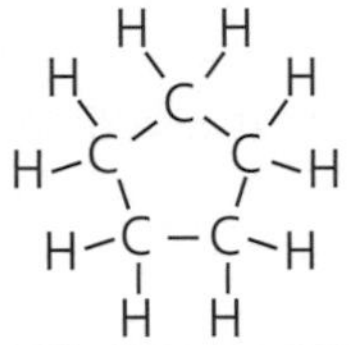
cyclohexane	C_6H_{12}	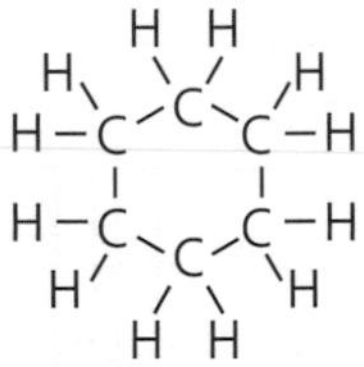

Alkenes and **cycloalkanes** form different homologous series. Both have the same **general formula** C_nH_{2n} but are different series as they have different chemical properties. Cycloalkanes will not decolourise bromine solution but alkenes will. If you were given a compound with the formula C_3H_6 you would use bromine solution to find out if it was propene or cyclopropane. Propene will decolourise the bromine solution but the cyclopropane will not.

Isomers are compounds with the **same molecular** formula but **different structural** formula. Propene and cyclopropane, for example, are isomers.

There is only one structural formula for methane, ethane and propane but all other alkanes have more than one possible structure. Shown alongside are the two structural formulae for butane:

Isomers of butane

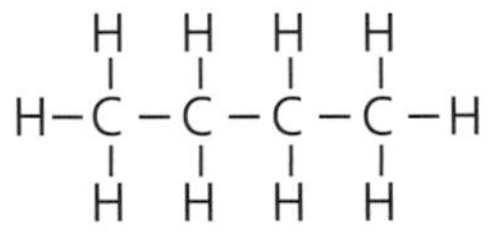

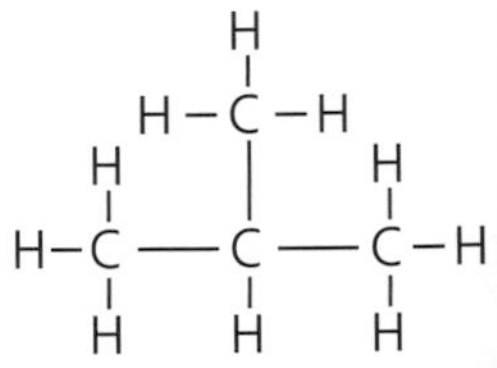

These two chemicals are isomers. Both structures have the same molecular formula C_4H_{10}. The first structural formula shows 4 carbon atoms in a row but the second structural formula has only three in a row and a branch.

continued

Look out for

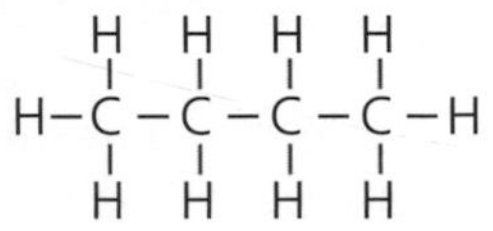

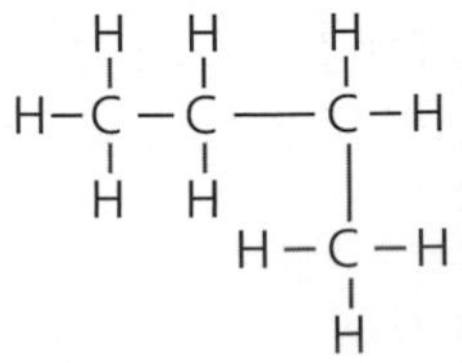

When you are dealing with alkanes you need to find the longest continuous chain of carbon atoms. For example, butane can be drawn in the two ways shown.

These two are **not** isomers of one another as they have the same structural formula. Both have 4 carbon atoms in a **row**. Compare these two structures with the two isomers of butane shown above.

What you should know at Credit level – continued

Butene has three alkene isomers as well as one cycloalkane isomer.

All four of these are isomers of one another. They have the same molecular formula of C_4H_8 but different structures. Changing the position of the double bond in an alkene can create an isomer.

Note that butane and butene are **not** isomers of one another. They have different molecular formulae.

Cracking an alkane produces a mixture of saturated and unsaturated products. **There are not enough hydrogen atoms in the alkane to make only saturated products.**

$$C_{20}H_{42} \rightarrow C_8H_{18} + C_8H_{16} + C_4H_8$$

saturated   saturated   unsaturated   unsaturated

Using a catalyst in cracking allows the reaction to take place at a lower temperature.

Look out for

Note that cycloalkanes and alkenes with the same molecular formula are isomers of one another even although they belong to different homologous series.

Balanced equations are part of the Credit syllabus. Many pupils find these difficult but it is a question of practice and confidence. Do not let this part of the course get you down!

Writing a balanced equation can be done in a series of steps.

First you need to know the reactants and products and write a word equation. For example ethene reacts with oxygen to make carbon dioxide and water.

Step 1 – Write the word equation.

$$\text{ethene} + \text{oxygen} \rightarrow \text{carbon dioxide} + \text{water}$$

Step 2 – Convert the words to formulae. At this step it is **vital** that the formulae are **correct**. Remember that oxygen is a diatomic element.

$$C_2H_4 + O_2 \rightarrow CO_2 + H_2O$$

Once you have the correct formulae you cannot alter them but use numbers in front of the formulae to balance the numbers of atoms of each element.

Step 3 – Balance each element in turn.

There are two C atoms on the left but only one on the right. So, put a 2 in front of the CO_2.

There are four H atoms on the left but two on the right. So, put a 2 in front of the H_2O.

$$C_2H_4 + O_2 \rightarrow 2CO_2 + 2H_2O$$

This balances the C and H but the O has now to be balanced. There are two O atoms on the left but now six on the right. So put a 3 in front of the O_2.

$$C_2H_4 + 3O_2 \rightarrow 2CO_2 + 2H_2O$$

Now the equation is balanced.

Credit question 1

The grid shows the formula for some hydrocarbons.

A	B	C
$CH_3-CH-CH_3$ $\quad\quad\; \mid$ $\quad\quad CH_3$	CH_2 H_2C-CH_2	$CH_3-CH_2-CH_2-CH_3$

D	E	F
H_3C $\quad\;\; \diagdown$ $\quad\quad C=CH_2$ $\quad\;\; \diagup$ H_3C	H_2C-CH_2 $\;\mid\quad\;\; \mid$ H_2C-CH_2	$H_3C\diagdown\quad\quad\diagup H$ $\quad\;\; C=C$ $H\diagup\quad\quad\diagdown H$

(a) Identify the **two** hydrocarbons with the general formula C_nH_{2n} which do **not** react quickly with bromine solution.

A	Ⓑ	C
D	Ⓔ	F

(b) Identify the two isomers of $CH_2= CH - CH_2 - CH_3$.

A	B	C
Ⓓ	Ⓔ	F

The first thing to do here is work out the molecular formula for all the hydrocarbons in the grid. Write them onto the grid. This should allow you to see that A and C do not fit into the formula C_nH_{2n}. You also need to know that the answer cannot be the compounds in boxes D and F as these two are both alkenes and would rapidly decolourise bromine solution. That leaves B and E as the answers. You can see that these are both cycloalkanes. Cycloalkanes are saturated so will not rapidly react with bromine solution.

Isomers have the same molecular formula but different structures. This molecule has the formula C_4H_8. Your answers must have the same formula. You should already have worked out the formulae for all the boxes in the grid. You can see that B and F only have three carbon atoms so cannot be correct. A and C have 10 hydrogen atoms so they cannot be correct.

Credit question 2

Hydrocarbons are compounds made from hydrogen and carbon only.

A	B	C
$\;\; H\;\; H$ $\;\;\mid\;\;\;\mid$ $H-C-C-H$ $\;\;\mid\;\;\;\mid$ $\;\; H\;\; H$	$\;\; H\;\; H\;\; H\;\; H$ $\;\;\mid\;\;\;\mid\;\;\;\mid\;\;\;\mid$ $H-C-C-C-C-H$ $\;\;\mid\;\;\;\mid\;\;\;\mid\;\;\;\mid$ $\;\; H\;\; H\;\; H\;\; H$	$\quad H\;\; H$ $\quad\; \diagup C\diagdown$ $H-C-C-H$ $\;\;\mid\quad\;\mid$ $\;\; H\quad H$

D	E	F
$H\quad\quad\quad H$ $\;\diagdown\quad\quad\;\mid$ $\;\; C=C-C-H$ $\;\diagup\quad\;\mid\;\;\;\mid$ $H\quad\; H\;\; H$	$\quad\;\; H\;\; H$ $\quad H\diagdown C\diagup H$ $H-C\quad\; C-H$ $\;\;\mid\quad\quad\mid$ $H-C-C-H$ $\quad\mid\;\;\;\mid$ $\quad H\;\; H$	$H\quad\quad\; H\;\; H$ $\;\diagdown\quad\;\;\mid\;\;\;\mid$ $\;\; C=C-C-C-H$ $\;\diagup\quad\;\;\mid\;\;\;\mid\;\;\;\mid$ $H\quad\quad H\;\; H\;\; H$

(a) Identify the hydrocarbon which reacts with hydrogen to form propane.

A	B	C
Ⓓ	E	F

Alkenes undergo addition reactions with hydrogen. The hydrogen molecule adds across the double bond. Box D contains propene C_3H_6. When hydrogen adds on this makes C_3H_8 or propane.

(b) Identify the **two** isomers.

A	B	Ⓒ
Ⓓ	E	F

(c) Identify the hydrocarbon which is the first member of a homologous series.

A	B	Ⓒ
D	E	F

Cyclopropane is the first member of the cycloalkanes.

You need to know that isomers are compounds with the same molecular formula but different structures. Work out the molecular formula for the hydrocarbons in the grid. Write the formula onto the grid. You don't need to do this for boxes A and E as there is only one entry with two carbon atoms A, and one with five, E. B and F have the same number of carbon atoms but different numbers of hydrogen atoms. You should see that C and D have the same formula but different structures.

Credit question 3

Dienes form a homologous series of hydrocarbons which contain two double bonds per molecule.

$$H \quad H \qquad H$$
$$C = C - C = C$$
$$H \qquad H \quad H$$

buta–1,3–diene

$$H \quad H \qquad H \quad H$$
$$C = C - C = C - C - H$$
$$H \qquad H \qquad H$$

penta–1,3–diene

$$H \quad H \qquad H \quad H \quad H$$
$$C = C - C = C - C - C - H$$
$$H \qquad H \qquad H \quad H$$

hexa–1,3–diene

(a) What is meant by the term "homologous series?"

A homologous series is a series of compounds, with **similar chemical properties** and for which a **general formula** can be written.

You need both parts of this definition to gain marks in a question.

(b) What is the general formula for dienes?

The general formula is C_nH_{2n-2}.

(c) What is the molecular formula of the compound produced by the complete reaction of hepta–1,3–diene and bromine?

The molecular formula is $C_7H_{12}Br_4$.

To work out the General formula calculate the molecular formula for each of the examples given in the question. This gives you C_4H_6, C_5H_8, C_6H_{12}. Now you need to see how to link the number of carbon atoms and the number of hydrogen atoms. If you double the number of carbon atoms and subtract 2 you will get the number of hydrogen atoms. This gives the General formula as C_nH_{2n-2}. Make sure that you write the n and 2n-2 **below** the line.

When an unsaturated hydrocarbon reacts with bromine solution a bromine molecule adds across the double bond. In this molecule there are **two** double bonds so that **two molecules of bromine** will add on.

(d) Draw a full structural formula for an **isomer** of buta–1,3–diene.

$$H-\overset{\displaystyle H}{\underset{\displaystyle H}{C}}-C\equiv C-\overset{\displaystyle H}{\underset{\displaystyle H}{C}}-H \qquad \overset{\displaystyle H}{\underset{\displaystyle H}{C}}=C=\overset{\displaystyle H}{C}-\overset{\displaystyle H}{\underset{\displaystyle H}{C}}-H$$

There are a number of possible answers here. Two possible answers are shown. Your answer must have the molecular formula C_4H_6. Remember that carbon forms 4 bonds and hydrogen forms 1 bond.

Look out for

Addition reactions. In an addition reaction one diatomic molecule adds across each double bond. It does not matter where the double bond is. e.g.

Br_2 +   but–2–ene   →   2,3dibromobutane

$$\underset{\displaystyle H\ H\ H\ H}{\overset{\displaystyle H\quad\quad H}{H-C-C=C-C-H}} \xrightarrow{\quad Br-Br \quad} \underset{\displaystyle H\ H\ H\ H}{\overset{\displaystyle H\ Br\ Br\ H}{H-C-C-C-C-H}}$$

Where there are two double bonds two diatomic molecules will be added. For example if buta–1,3–diene as shown in question three is added to bromine solution the product will have the molecular formula $C_4H_6Br_4$ and the structural formula

$$\underset{\displaystyle H\ H\ Br\ Br}{\overset{\displaystyle Br\ Br\ H\ H}{H-C-C-C-C-H}}$$

Properties of substances

What you should know at General **level...**

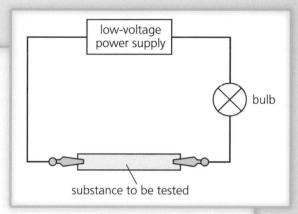

low-voltage power supply

bulb

substance to be tested

A **current** of electricity is a flow of charged particles.

A substance which:

- allows a current of electricity to pass through it is called an **electrical conductor.**
- does not allow a current of electricity to pass through it is called an **electrical insulator** or **non–conductor**.

The electrical conductivity of a substance can be tested using the circuit on the right:

If the bulb lights up the substance conducts electricity. A buzzer or ammeter could also be used in place of the bulb in this experiment.

Metal elements conduct electricity in the solid and liquid (molten) states.

Most non-metal elements do not conduct electricity in any state. One exception to this general rule is the non-metal **carbon**, in the form of graphite.

Covalent compounds do not conduct electricity in the solid or liquid (molten) states nor when they are in solution.

Ionic compounds – compounds in which a metal and non-metal are usually bonded together – do not conduct electricity in the solid state but do conduct in the molten state and in solution.

To conduct electricity, a substance must contain **charged particles** which are able to **move**. The **moving charged particles** which allow:

- metals to conduct are **free electrons.**
- ionic compounds to conduct when molten or in solution are called **ions**. Although solid ionic compounds contain charged particles (ions) they do not conduct since the **ions can't move**. Ions are formed when atoms lose or gain electrons. For example when a magnesium atom (Mg) loses two electrons it forms the magnesium ion Mg^{2+} and when a chlorine atom (Cl) gains one electron it forms the chloride ion Cl^-. In general metal ions are positively charged and non-metal ions are negatively charged.

Non-metal elements and covalent compounds are made up of molecules and since molecules have no charge these substances cannot conduct electricity.

The **electrical conductivities of substances** are summarised in the following table:

Substance	Type of element present	Bonding	Electrical conductivity as			Conducting particles
			solid	**liquid/molten**	**solution**	
Elements	metal	metallic	✓	✓	–	free electrons
	non-metal	covalent	✗	✗	✗	none
Compounds	non-metal/non-metal	covalent	✗	✗	✗	none
	metal/non-metal	ionic	✗	✓	✓	moving ions

✓ = conducts electricity ✗ = does not conduct electricity

continued

Covalent compounds:

▸ are those in which non-metals are bonded together.

▸ are formed when non-metal atoms share electrons.

▸ normally exist as gases or liquids at room temperature and have low melting and boiling points. The few covalent compounds that exist in the solid state at room temperature generally have low melting points. The melting and boiling points of some covalent compounds can be found on page 6 of the data booklet.

▸ are generally insoluble in water but usually dissolve in other solvents such as carbon tetrachloride, propanone and hexane. These solvents are examples of **non-aqueous solvents**. The covalent compounds in oil and grease for example are insoluble in water but dissolve in non-aqueous solvents.

Ionic compounds:

▸ are usually formed when a metal combines with a non-metal(s).

▸ are formed when electrons are transferred from the metal atoms to the non-metal atoms.

▸ exist as a lattice of oppositely charged ions. For example the sodium chloride lattice is illustrated to the right. Each positively charged sodium ion is surrounded by negatively charged chloride ions and vice versa.

▸ are generally soluble in water but insoluble in non-aqueous solvents. When an ionic compound dissolves in water the lattice breaks up completely. You can check if an ionic compound is soluble in water by looking up page 5 of your data booklet.

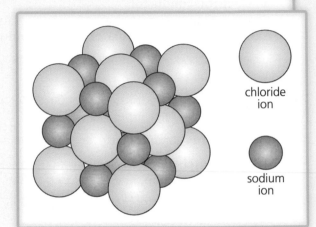

chloride ion

sodium ion

▸ exist in the solid state at room temperature and have high melting points and boiling points. The melting and boiling points of some ionic compounds are shown on page 6 of the data booklet.

Atoms form ions by losing or gaining electrons.

▸ Positively charged metal ions are formed when metal atoms lose electrons.

▸ Negatively charged non-metal ions are formed when non-metal atoms gain electrons.

The ions that metal and non-metal atoms form depend on which group they occupy in the Periodic Table.

Group in Periodic Table	1	2	3	5	6	7
Ion formula	M^+	M^{2+}	M^{3+}	X^{3-}	X^{2-}	X^-

M = metal, **X** = non-metal

Some ions contain more than one kind of atom and these can be called **group ions**. For example the **sulphate ion** is a group ion and has the formula SO_4^{2-}.

You will notice that the sulphate ion contains **one** sulphur atom and **four** oxygen atoms and it has an overall charge of 2−. The formulae for a number of group ions can be found on page 6 of the data booklet. All the group ions on page 6 have names ending in **-ate** or **-ite** apart from the **ammonium ion** (NH_4^+) and the **hydroxide ion** (OH^-).

Chemical formulae for ionic compounds can be written in the following way.

Example 1: magnesium chloride

▸ Use the Periodic Table to work out the formula for each ion. Magnesium is in Group 2 and will form the Mg^{2+} ion. Chlorine is in Group 7 and will form the Cl^- ion.

▸ Work out how many of each ion is needed to make the overall charge zero. A magnesium ion has a 2+ charge and a chloride ion has a 1− charge therefore two **Cl⁻** ions are needed for each **Mg²⁺** ion.

continued

What you should know at General level – continued

▶ Write the chemical formula for the compound based on the number of ions of each element present and add the state symbol. **MgCl$_2$(s)** for **solid** magnesium chloride and **MgCl$_2$(aq)** for a **solution** of magnesium chloride. The state symbol **(aq)** means in **aq**ueous solution – a solution of the ionic compound dissolved in water.

Example 2: **sodium carbonate**

▶ In this case, the **-ate** ending in the name indicates that a group ion is present. By looking up page 6 of the data booklet you will find that the carbonate ion has the formula **CO$_3{}^{2-}$**. Sodium is in Group 1 and will form the **Na$^+$** ion.

▶ Since the sodium ion has a 1+ charge and the carbonate ion has a 2– charge then two **Na$^+$** ions are needed to balance the charge on each **CO$_3{}^{2-}$** ion.

▶ The chemical formulae are **Na$_2$CO$_3$(s)** for solid sodium carbonate and **Na$_2$CO$_3$(aq)** for a solution of sodium carbonate.

An **electrolyte** is a solution or melt of an ionic compound. It will conduct electricity since it contains ions which are free to move.

Electrolysis is the passage of a current of electricity through an electrolyte.

The diagram shows the electrolysis of the electrolyte copper chloride solution.

▶ The copper ions (Cu^{2+}) have a positive charge and are attracted to the negative electrode since opposite charges attract. The copper ions are changed into copper atoms which collect on the electrode.

▶ The negatively charged chloride ions (Cl$^-$) are attracted to the positive electrode and are changed into molecules of chlorine gas.

▶ The electrical energy supplied has chemically changed the copper chloride solution into copper and chlorine.

▶ The electrodes are made of carbon in the form of graphite. Graphite is a suitable electrode material because it conducts electricity but will not react with the electrolyte.

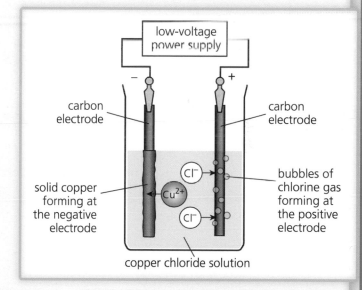

▶ Unlike an electrolyte, when a metal conducts electricity, the electrical energy supplied does **not** chemically change the metal.

Most ionic compounds are white in the solid state and dissolve in water to form colourless solutions. However some ionic compounds are **coloured** and dissolve in water to form coloured solutions. For example:

Compound	Positive ion	Negative ion	Colour
potassium chloride	potassium ion	chloride ion	colourless
copper chloride	copper ion	chloride ion	blue
potassium permanganate	potassium ion	permanganate ion	purple

continued

What you should know at General level – continued

The colour of an ionic compound depends on the colours of the ions it contains.

▸ Potassium chloride is colourless and this indicates that both potassium ions and chloride ions are colourless.
▸ Copper chloride is blue. We know chloride ions are colourless so it must be the copper ions that are blue.
▸ Potassium permanganate is purple and as potassium ions are colourless it must be the permanganate ions that are purple.

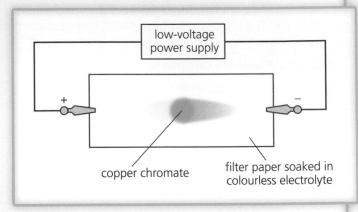

The diagram on the right shows what happens when a solution of the green coloured ionic compound copper chromate is electrolysed.

▸ A blue colour moves towards the negative electrode since the blue copper ions are positively charged.
▸ A yellow colour moves towards the positive electrode since the yellow chromate ions are negatively charged.

General question 1

A technician set up an experiment to investigate electrical conductivity.

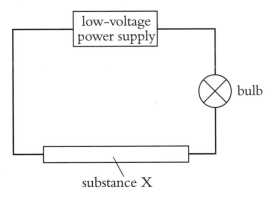

	Substance X
A	molten metal
B	covalent liquid
C	ionic solution
D	ionic solid
E	solid metal

Identify the **two** experiments in which the bulb would **not** light.

The answers are B and D.

Look out for

The charged particles that allow metals and solutions/melts of ionic compounds to conduct are often mixed up. Remember that **metals** conduct because they have free **electrons**. A solution or melt of an **ionic compound** conducts because it contains **ions which can move**.

*The bulb will not light if the substance does **not** conduct electricity. You will remember that metals conduct electricity in both the solid and molten states eliminating A and E. Ionic compounds do not conduct electricity in the solid state but do conduct in solution so C can be eliminated but D must be one of the answers. Covalent substances do not conduct electricity in any state and so B must be the other answer.*

General question 2

Martin set up the following experiment.

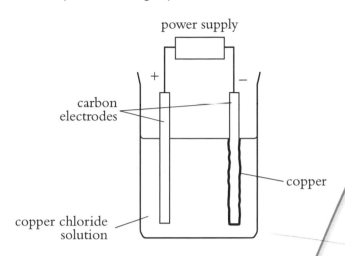

power supply

carbon electrodes

copper

copper chloride solution

Looking at the diagram you can see that a current of electricity is being passed through copper chloride solution and changes have taken place at the electrodes.

What you have to realise here is that copper chloride is an ionic compound and contains ions – copper ions and chloride ions. Copper ions are positively charged since they are metal ions.

(a) What type of experiment did Martin carry out?

He performed an electrolysis experiment.

(b) Why does copper form at the negative electrode?

Opposite charges attract therefore the positively charged copper ions are attracted to the negative electrode where they change into copper atoms.

(c) What would you see happening at the positive electrode?

You would see bubbles of chlorine gas being given off at the positive electrode.

(d) Carbon is unreactive and insoluble in water.

Give another reason why it is suitable for use as electrodes.

Carbon conducts electricity.

The negatively charged chloride ions would be attracted to the positive electrode and change into chlorine molecules.

Look out for

You are often given information about the electrical conductivities of substances and then asked to work out the type of bonding in these substances. It is worthwhile to remember that:

▶ **metals** are the **only** substances that conduct in the **solid** state.
▶ **covalent substances** do **not** conduct in **any state**.
▶ **ionic compounds** conduct **only** in **molten** state and in **solution, never** in the **solid** state.

What you should know at Credit level...

Atoms form ions in order to become more stable. They can achieve this stability by getting the same electron arrangement as a noble gas. For example:

▶ calcium is in Group 2 of the Periodic Table and has an electron arrangement of 2, 8, 8, 2. Its nearest noble gas is argon which has an electron arrangement of 2, 8, 8. This means that a calcium atom has to lose two electrons when it forms the calcium ion, Ca^{2+}.
▶ nitrogen is in Group 5 of the Periodic Table and has an electron arrangement of 2, 5. Its nearest noble gas is neon which has an electron arrangement of 2, 8. This means that a nitrogen atom has to gain three electrons when it forms the nitride ion, N^{3-}.

continued

What you should know at Credit level – continued

The ions formed by metal and non-metal atoms are summarised in the following table:

Group in Periodic Table	1	2	3	5	6	7
Number of outer electrons	1	2	3	5	6	7
Number of electrons to be lost	1	2	3			
Number of electrons to be gained				3	2	1
Ion formula	M^+	M^{2+}	M^{3+}	X^{3-}	X^{2-}	X^-

M = metal, **X** = non-metal

Some elements, particularly the transition elements, can form **ions with different charges**. In these cases the charge is shown in **Roman numerals** after the elements name. For example:

▶ in copper(I) oxide the charge on the **copper(I)** ion is 1+ (**Cu^+**).
▶ in iron(III) chloride the charge on the **iron(III)** ion is 3+ (**Fe^{3+}**).

Notice that the Roman numeral simply gives the charge on the ion – there is no need to look up the position of the element in the Periodic Table.

Look out for

Given the chemical formula for an ionic compound it can be quite difficult to work out the charge on each ion. In one recent question candidates were asked to work out the charge on the iron ion in the compound Fe_2O_3. We know that oxygen is in Group 6 and forms the O^{2-} ion. There are three O^{2-} ions in the formula so the total negative charge must be 6–. This implies that the total positive charge must be 6+ and since there are two iron ions in the formula each one must have a charge of 3+.

In writing formulae for ionic compounds containing more than one group ion then brackets must be used. Consider for example, **iron(III) sulphate**:

▶ iron(III) sulphate contains the **Fe^{3+}** ion and the **SO_4^{2-}** ion.
▶ to balance the charge two **Fe^{3+}** ions and three **SO_4^{2-}** ions are needed and so the formulae will be **$Fe_2(SO_4)_3(s)$** for solid iron(III) sulphate and **$Fe_2(SO_4)_3(aq)$** for iron(III) sulphate solution.

Sometimes you are asked to write the **ionic formula** for a compound. In such a formula the ion charges **must** be shown. If there are two or more of one type of ion the formula for that ion **must** be enclosed in brackets. For example the ionic formulae for:

▶ iron(III) sulphate would be **$(Fe^{3+})_2(SO_4^{2-})_3(s)$** or **$(Fe^{3+})_2(SO_4^{2-})_3(aq)$**.
▶ calcium hydroxide would be **$Ca^{2+}(OH^-)_2(s)$** or **$Ca^{2+}(OH^-)_2(aq)$**.

Ionic compounds exist in the solid state at room temperature and consist of a lattice of oppositely charged ions (see page 48). The bonds between these ions are called **ionic bonds** and they are very strong. When melting or boiling ionic compounds these strong bonds have to be broken which explains why they have **high melting and boiling points**.

The vast majority of **covalent substances** adopt a structure called a **covalent molecular structure** which is a collection of small, separate molecules. The bonds **inside** the separate molecules are strong covalent bonds and the bonds **between** the molecules are very weak. The diagram at the top of page 53 shows what happens when a covalent molecular substance is heated.

continued

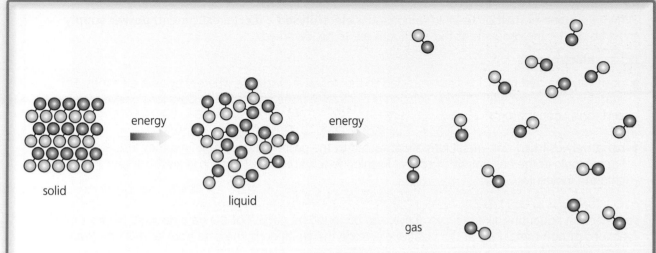

solid

energy

liquid

energy

gas

When a covalent molecular substance melts the molecules move slightly apart and when it boils they move very far apart. In melting and boiling such a substance only the bonds between the molecules are broken, not the covalent bonds inside the molecules. Since the bonds between the molecules are weak, very little energy is needed to break them and this explains why **covalent molecular substances** have **low melting and boiling points**.

A few covalent substances, like carbon (diamond) and silicon dioxide, have very high melting and boiling points. They adopt a **covalent network structure**:

A covalent network substance consists of one **giant molecule** in which the atoms are joined by strong covalent bonds – there are no weak bonds present. On melting and boiling such a substance the strong covalent bonds have to be broken. This requires a great deal of energy and explains why **covalent network substances** have **high melting and boiling points**.

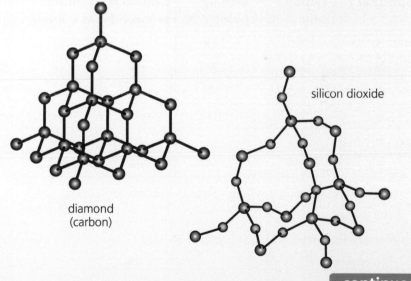

silicon dioxide

diamond
(carbon)

continued

Look out for

Usually ionic compounds are made up of a metal combined with a non-metal but there are exceptions to this general rule. You need to know the properties of a compound before you can be definite about the bonding present. Take tin iodide (SnI_4) for example. It was formed from the metal tin and the non-metal iodine and at first glance looks as if it should be ionic. But tin iodide does **not** conduct electricity in the molten state. This implies that the bonding is covalent and **not** ionic. Now that you have established that it is covalent how can you tell whether it has a covalent molecular structure or a covalent network structure? Again you turn to the properties to get the answer. Tin iodide is a solid at room temperature but it has a low melting point and from this fact you can deduce that it has a covalent molecular structure.

What you should know at Credit level – continued

When a solution or melt of an ionic compound is **electrolysed** a **d.c.** (direct current) **power supply** must be used if the products at the electrodes are to be identified.

During **electrolysis:**

▶ positively charged metal ions are attracted to the negative electrode where they gain electrons. For example when copper(II) chloride solution is electrolysed (see page 49) the Cu^{2+} ions gain electrons and form copper atoms.

$$Cu^{2+}(aq) + 2e^- \rightarrow Cu(s)$$

▶ negatively charged non-metal ions are attracted to the positive electrode where they lose electrons. For example in the electrolysis of copper(II) chloride solution the Cl^- ions lose electrons and form chlorine molecules.

$$2Cl^-(aq) \rightarrow Cl_2(g) + 2e^-$$

Ion–electron equations, like the two above, can be found on page 7 of the data booklet. Notice that for reactions of non-metal ions at the positive electrode the equation in the data booklet must be reversed.

Credit question 1

The table contains information about some substances.

Substance	Melting point / °C	Boiling point / °C	Conducts as a solid	Conducts as a liquid
A	1700	2230	no	no
B	605	1305	no	yes
C	−13	77	no	no
D	801	1413	no	yes
E	181	1347	yes	yes
F	−39	357	yes	yes

(a) Identify the substance which exists as covalent molecules.

The answer is **C**.

(b) Identify the metal which is liquid at 25°C.

The answer is **F**.

You know that covalent substances do not conduct electricity in any state therefore A or C must be the answer. Covalent substances can have two different types of structure –covalent molecular and covalent network. The substance you are trying to identify has a covalent molecular structure. When such a substance is melted or boiled the bonds between the molecules are broken and since these are weak very little energy will be needed. As a result the melting and boiling points will be low.

Credit question 2

The Periodic Table lists all known elements. The grid shows the names of six common elements.

A oxygen	B calcium	C aluminium
D sodium	E magnesium	F fluorine

From recall you know that metals conduct in both the solid and molten states, so the answer must be E or F. At 25°C E will be a solid as its melting point of 181°C is above 25°C. F must be the answer and this is confirmed by the fact that 25°C lies between its melting point and boiling point.

(a) Identify the element which can form ions with the same electron arrangement as argon.

A	Ⓑ	C
D	E	F

By looking up page 1 of the data booklet you can see that the element which is nearest to argon is calcium. It has the electron arrangement 2, 8, 8, 2. In forming an ion it loses two electrons and so the calcium ion will have the electron arrangement 2, 8, 8 which is the same as that of argon.

(b) Identify the **two** elements which form an ionic compound with the formula of the type XY_3, where **X** is the metal.

A	B	Ⓒ
D	E	Ⓕ

The easiest way of tackling this question is to write the ionic formula for XY_3. The X ion must have a charge of 3+ and the Y ion must have a charge of 1− giving the ionic formula $X^{3+}(Y^-)_3$. To form the X^{3+} ion X must be in Group 3 of the Periodic Table and to form the Y^- ion Y must be in Group 7. Aluminium is in Group 3 and fluorine is in Group 7.

Credit question 3

Molten lead bromide can be broken up into its elements by passing electricity through it.

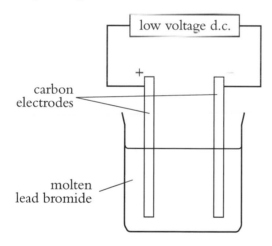

(a) Bromine is released at the positive electrode.

Write an ion–electron equation for the formation of bromine.

You may wish to use the data booklet to help you.

$2Br^- \rightarrow Br_2 + 2e^-$

Molten lead bromide contains lead ions and bromide ions and it is the negatively charged bromide ions which change into bromine molecules at the positive electrode. You then look up page 7 of the data booklet to find the appropriate ion–electron equation. It is the third one from the bottom and you will notice that it has to be reversed since you need the bromide ions to be the reactants and the bromine molecules to be the products.

Look out for

When writing ion–electron equations make sure you get them the right way round. For example when copper(II) chloride solution is electrolysed chlorine gas is formed at the positive electrode. You can find the appropriate ion–electron equation on page 7 of the data booklet but do you write it as:

$Cl_2(g) + 2e^- \rightarrow 2Cl^-(aq)$ or $2Cl^-(aq) \rightarrow Cl_2(g) + 2e^-$?

You are told that chlorine gas is formed at the positive electrode which means that $Cl_2(g)$ is a **product** of the reaction and as such must appear to the right of the arrow. So the correct ion–electron equation is:

$2Cl^-(aq) \rightarrow Cl_2(g) + 2e^-$

(b) Why do ionic compounds, like lead bromide, conduct electricity when molten but not when solid?

In the solid state the ions cannot move and therefore cannot carry a current of electricity. In the molten state the ions can move and can carry a current of electricity.

Although lead bromide contains ions both in the solid and molten states it is only when the lattice breaks up on melting that the ions can move.

Credit question 4

Many ionic compounds are coloured.

Compound	Colour
nickel(II) nitrate	green
nickel(II) sulphate	green
potassium permanganate	purple
potassium sulphate	colourless

(a) Using information in the table, state the colour of the potassium ion.

The potassium ion is colourless.

(b) Write the **ionic** formula for nickel(II) nitrate.

$Ni^{2+}(NO_3^-)_2(s)$

You will recall that the colour of an ionic compound depends on the colours of the ions it contains. There are two potassium compounds in the list – potassium permanganate and potassium chloride. Since potassium permanganate is purple then either the potassium ion or the permanganate ion must be purple. If the potassium ion was purple then potassium sulphate would be purple. But potassium sulphate is colourless so the potassium ion must be colourless.

*The first important thing to notice is that the **ionic** formula is required. This means that the charges on the ions must be shown. The Roman numeral (II) tells you that the nickel(II) ion has a 2+ charge so its formula must be Ni^{2+}. The –ate ending in the name indicates that the nitrate ion is a group ion and by looking up page 4 of the data booklet you find that its formula is NO_3^-. You will need two nitrate ions for each nickel(II) ion in order to balance up the charge. The ionic formula for nickel(II) nitrate is $Ni^{2+}(NO_3^-)_2(s)$. Notice that you must have brackets round the nitrate ion since two of them are present. The formula without the state symbol would also be an acceptable answer. i.e. $Ni^{2+}(NO_3^-)_2$.*

Look out for

Writing **ionic formulae** often proves difficult. Remember to include the charge on each ion and if necessary, brackets. Consider calcium bromide. Calcium is in Group 2 and forms the Ca^{2+} ion. Bromine is in Group 7 and forms the Br^- ion. Two Br^- ions are required for each Ca^{2+} ion in order to balance up the charge. The ionic formula for calcium bromide is **$Ca^{2+}(Br^-)_2(s)$** and **not** $Ca^{2+}Br_2^-(s)$

(c) A student set up the following experiment to investigate the colour of the ions in copper(II) chromate.

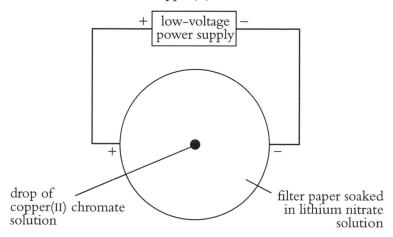

drop of copper(II) chromate solution

filter paper soaked in lithium nitrate solution

The student made the following observations.

Observations
yellow colour moves to the positive electrode
blue colour moves to the negative electrode

(i) State the colour of the chromate ion.

The chromate ion is yellow.

Metal ions like the copper(II) ion are positively charged, so the chromate ion must be negatively charged. It will be attracted to the positive electrode.

(ii) Lithium nitrate solution is used as the electrolyte.

What is the purpose of an electrolyte?

It is to complete the circuit by allowing the movement of ions.

As a solution of an ionic compound, an electrolyte is able to carry a current of electricity.

(iii) Suggest why lithium phosphate can **not** be used as the electrolyte in this experiment.

You may wish to use the data booklet to help you.

Lithium phosphate is insoluble.

Lithium phosphate is ionic and so has the potential to form an electrolyte. If it was insoluble in water then it could not form an electrolyte. Check on page 5 of the data booklet to confirm that it is insoluble.

Acids and alkalis

What you should know at General level...

The **pH scale** is a measure of how **acidic** or **alkaline** a solution is and ranges from 0 to 14.

The **pH of a solution** can be found by adding pH paper or pH indicator such as universal indictor to the solution and matching the colour of the paper or indicator to one on a pH colour chart like the one below:

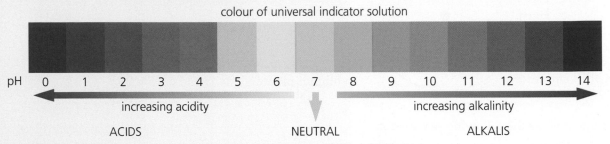

colour of universal indicator solution

pH 0 1 2 3 4 5 6 7 8 9 10 11 12 13 14

increasing acidity   increasing alkalinity

ACIDS   NEUTRAL   ALKALIS

Acids have a **pH less than 7** and the **lower the pH** the **more acidic** it is.

Alkalis have a **pH greater than 7** and the **higher the pH** the **more alkaline** it is.

Pure water and neutral solutions have a **pH equal to 7**.

Some **common acids and alkalis** used **in the home and in the lab** are shown in the following table:

Household acids	Household alkalis	Lab acids	Lab alkalis
vinegar	baking soda	hydrochloric acid	sodium hydroxide solution
lemonade	oven cleaner	sulphuric acid	ammonia solution
fruit juices	dishwashing powder	nitric acid	calcium hydroxide solution

Acids are formed when **soluble non-metal oxides** dissolve in water. For example **sulphur dioxide** dissolves in rain water to form **acid rain**.

Acid rain can have a devastating effect on the environment. It can:

▸ kill plants such as trees and make soil so acidic that plants won't grow in it.
▸ kill animals like fish when lochs are polluted.
▸ damage structures made of iron and steel by reacting with the iron.
▸ damage statues and buildings made of marble and limestone by reacting with the calcium carbonate in these materials.

Alkalis are formed when **soluble metal oxides** or **soluble metal hydroxides** dissolve in water. For example:

▸ sodium oxide reacts with water to form the alkali sodium hydroxide solution.
▸ calcium hydroxide dissolves in water to form the alkali calcium hydroxide solution, commonly called lime water.

As they conduct electricity both **acidic and alkaline solutions contain ions**. **Water** also conducts electricity but only very slightly – this implies that it **contains ions** but their **concentration is very small**.

The **main ions** in:

▸ **acidic solutions** are **hydrogen ions, H⁺(aq)** ions.
▸ **alkaline solutions** are **hydroxide ions, OH⁻(aq)** ions.

continued

What you should know at General level – continued

The presence of hydrogen ions in acidic solutions can be demonstrated by electrolysing an acid such as dilute sulphuric acid (as shown on the right):

The positively charged hydrogen ions ($H^+(aq)$) are attracted to the negative electrode where they are converted into hydrogen gas.

You can show that the gas collected in the test tube is hydrogen by applying the **test for hydrogen**:

When a **lighted splint** is placed in the mouth of the test tube the gas burns with a **squeaky pop** if it is hydrogen.

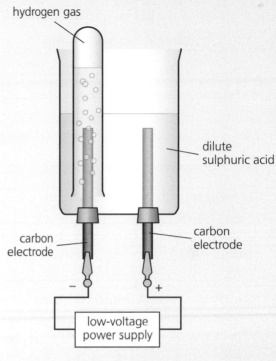

hydrogen gas

dilute sulphuric acid

carbon electrode

carbon electrode

low-voltage power supply

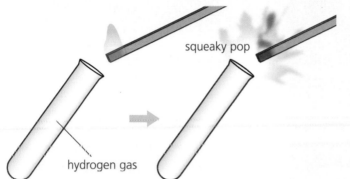

squeaky pop

hydrogen gas

When an:

▶ **acidic solution is diluted** by adding water its **pH increases towards 7** and it **becomes less acidic.**
▶ **alkaline solution is diluted** by adding water its **pH decreases towards 7** and it **becomes less alkaline**.

The following tables show the ions present in some common **acids and alkalis** and the **formulae** of these acids and alkalis.

Acid	Ions present	Formulae
hydrochloric	hydrogen ions and chloride ions	$HCl(aq)$ or $H^+(aq) + Cl^-(aq)$
nitric	hydrogen ions and nitrate ions	$HNO_3(aq)$ or $H^+(aq) + NO_3^-(aq)$
sulphuric	hydrogen ions and sulphate ions	$H_2SO_4(aq)$ or $2H^+(aq) + SO_4^{2-}(aq)$

Alkali	Ions present	Formulae
sodium hydroxide	sodium ions and hydroxide ions	$NaOH(aq)$ or $Na^+(aq) + OH^-(aq)$
potassium hydroxide	potassium ions and hydroxide ions	$KOH(aq)$ or $K^+(aq) + OH^-(aq)$
calcium hydroxide	calcium ions and hydroxide ions	$Ca(OH)_2(aq)$ or $Ca^{2+}(aq) + 2OH^-(aq)$

Look out for

The tests for hydrogen and oxygen are often confused. In testing for hydrogen a **lighted** splint is used and the gas burns with a squeaky pop. In testing for oxygen a **glowing** splint is used and the gas relights the glowing splint.

General question 1

The chart shows the pH of different substances.

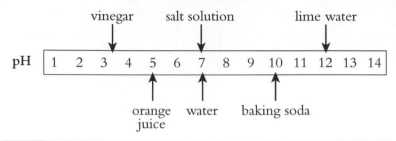

(a) Identify the **two** substances which are neutral.

A	Ⓑ	C
D	Ⓔ	F

(b) Identify the substance which is the most alkaline.

A	B	Ⓒ
D	E	F

You should remember that solutions with a pH of 7 are neutral.

Alkaline solutions have a pH greater than 7, and this narrows your choices to baking soda and lime water. From recall you know that the higher the pH the more alkaline the solution.

Provided you remember that soluble metal oxides and soluble metal hydroxides dissolve in water to give alkaline solutions, you quickly arrive at the answers A and B. You do not need to check that barium hydroxide and calcium oxide are soluble because in the introduction it says 'the grid shows compounds which dissolve in water'. This demonstrates that you need to take on board all the information in the question and not just the entries in the grid.

General question 2

The grid shows compounds which dissolve in water.

A barium hydroxide	B calcium oxide	C carbon dioxide
D potassium nitrate	E sodium chloride	F sulphur dioxide

(a) Identify the **two** compounds which produce alkaline solutions.

Ⓐ	Ⓑ	C
D	E	F

(b) Identify the substance which causes acid rain.

A	B	C
D	E	Ⓕ

Look out for

Make sure you remember that it is **non-metal** oxides (if soluble) that dissolve in water to form **acids** and that it is **metal** oxides and **metal** hydroxides (if soluble) that dissolve in water to form **alkalis**.

Acid rain is caused by sulphur dioxide dissolving in rain water. Nitrogen dioxide will also dissolve in rain water to give acid rain but it is not in the grid.

General question 3

Class 4A made some statements about the effect of adding water to an alkaline solution.

A	The pH of the solution will rise.
B	The solution will become more concentrated.
C	The pH of the solution will fall towards 7.
D	Adding water will have no effect on the solution.

Identify the correct statement.

The answer is C.

Adding water to the alkaline solution means that it is being diluted and its concentration will fall, eliminating B. You also know that in diluting an alkaline solution its pH will decrease towards 7, ruling out A but giving C as the correct answer. It is important to check out D just in case! You know that adding water to an alkaline solution lowers its pH and lowers its concentration, so D cannot be correct.

General question 4

Mr Clarke carried out an experiment with different elements. The workcard showed what he did.

1. Burn element in oxygen.

oxygen — burning element

2. Add water to oxide formed.

oxide and water

3. Add universal indicator.

universal indicator

4. Compare the colour of the indicator with a pH chart.

(a) (i) Complete the table showing the results Mr Clarke would have obtained.

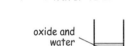

Name of oxide	pH of solution
carbon dioxide	4
sodium oxide	12
aluminium oxide	could not be measured

(ii) Suggest a reason why the pH of aluminium oxide could not be measured.
You may wish to use page 5 of the data booklet to help you.

It is insoluble in water.

(b) When an element burns, it reacts with oxygen to form an oxide. Write an equation, using symbols and formulae, for the reaction between sodium and oxygen. (There is no need to balance the equation.)

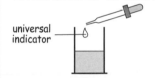

$Na + O_2 \rightarrow Na_2O$ or $Na(s) + O_2(g) \rightarrow Na_2O(s)$

Carbon dioxide is an oxide of a non-metal which means it will dissolve in water to give an acidic solution. Any pH less than 7 would be acceptable as an answer. By looking up page 5 of the data booklet you find that sodium oxide is soluble and since it is an oxide of a metal it will dissolve in water to give an alkaline solution. Any pH greater than 7 would be acceptable.

You might have expected aluminium oxide to have formed an alkaline solution since it is a metal oxide but if you look up page 5 of the data booklet you find that it doesn't dissolve in water.

The reactants are the elements sodium and oxygen and you will recall from Topic 4 that the formula for an element depends on whether it is diatomic or not. Sodium is not diatomic and so its formula is Na. Oxygen is diatomic and its formula is O_2. The product is sodium oxide and it is ionic. You will remember from Topic 7 that you need to first work out the charge on each ion. Sodium is in Group 1 and forms the Na^+ ion, while oxygen is in Group 6 and forms the O^{2-} ion. To balance the charge you need two Na^+ ions for each O^{2-} ion giving the formula for sodium oxide as Na_2O.

General question 5

Jack and Iona measured the pH of some fizzy drinks.

Drink	pH
Just Fizz	5
Fizz Alive	3
Jupiter	4

(a) Describe how you would use universal indicator to measure the pH of a fizzy drink.

Add a few drops of universal indicator to the fizzy drink, match the colour of the indicator to one of the colours on the pH colour chart and read off the pH.

(b) The more acidic the drink, the more likely it is to increase tooth decay.
Name the fizzy drink which would be most likely to increase tooth decay.

Fizz Alive.

(c) Name the ion present in **all** acidic solutions.

*The ion which is common to all acidic solutions is the **hydrogen** ion.*

Look out for

The lower the pH of an acid the **more** acidic it is but the lower the pH of an alkali the **less** alkaline it is.

What you should know at **Credit** level...

All aqueous solutions contain both **hydrogen ions** ($H^+(aq)$) **and hydroxide ions** ($OH^-(aq)$). It is the relative concentrations of these ions which decide whether a solution is neutral, acidic or alkaline.

▶ In **pure water** and in **neutral solutions**:
   concentration of $H^+(aq)$ ions = concentration of $OH^-(aq)$ ions
▶ In **acidic solutions**:
   concentration of $H^+(aq)$ ions is **greater** than concentration of $OH^-(aq)$ ions
▶ In **alkaline solutions**:
   concentration of $H^+(aq)$ ions is **less** than concentration of $OH^-(aq)$ ions

On **diluting**:

▶ an **acid** the concentration of its hydrogen ions decreases and it becomes less acidic.
▶ an **alkali** the concentration of its hydroxide ions decreases and it becomes less alkaline.

Look out for

As **pH increases** the concentration of $H^+(aq)$ **ions decreases** while the concentration of $OH^-(aq)$ **ions increases**. Similarly as **pH decreases** the concentration of $H^+(aq)$ **ions increases** while the concentration of $OH^-(aq)$ **ions decreases**.

The **relative formula mass** (RFM) of a substance can be found by writing the formula of the substance and then adding together the relative atomic masses (RAM) of all the atoms in that formula. (You can find relative atomic masses on page 4 of the data booklet.)

continued

What you should know at Credit level – continued

Example 1: Calculate the relative formula mass of carbon dioxide (CO_2).

formula $\qquad$ $\mathbf{CO_2}(g)$

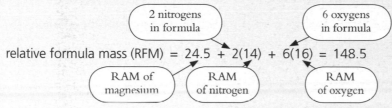

relative formula mass (RFM) = 12 + 2(16) = 44

Example 2: Calculate the relative formula mass of magnesium nitrate ($Mg(NO_3)_2$).

formula $\qquad$ $\mathbf{Mg(NO_3)_2}(s)$

The '**2**' in the formula implies that magnesium nitrate contains **two** nitrate ions (NO_3^-). This means that there are 2 nitrogens and 6 (2x3) oxygens present.

relative formula mass (RFM) = 24.5 + 2(14) + 6(16) = 148.5

Notice that relative formula mass, like relative atomic mass, has no units.

Chemists use the term **mole** to mean **an amount of substance**. It corresponds to the relative formula mass of the substance in grams and is known as the **gram formula mass** (**GFM**).

Example 3: Calculate the mass of one mole of calcium carbonate ($CaCO_3$).

$CaCO_3(s)$ GFM = 40 + 12 + 3(16) = 100 g

1 mole of calcium carbonate has a mass of 100 g.

Given the mass of a substance you must be able to work out the number of moles of the substance and vice versa.

Grams to moles:

Example 4: Calculate the number of moles of carbon dioxide in 1.1 g of carbon dioxide (CO_2).

$CO_2(g)$ GFM = 12 + 2(16) = 44 g

44 g $\longleftrightarrow$ 1 mol

1.1 g $\longleftrightarrow$ $\dfrac{1.1}{44} \times 1$

$\qquad = 0.025$ mol

Moles to grams:

Example 5: Calculate the mass of 2.5 mol of water (H_2O).

$H_2O(l)$ GFM = 2(1) + 16 = 18 g

1 mol $\longleftrightarrow$ 18 g

2.5 mol $\longleftrightarrow$ $\dfrac{2.5}{1} \times 18$

$\qquad = 45$ g

continued

What you should know at Credit level – continued

An aqueous solution is formed when a solute is dissolved in water and the **concentration of the solution** can be expressed as the **number of moles of solute per litre of solution (mol/l):**

$$\text{concentration}(C) = \frac{\text{number of moles of solute (n)}}{\text{volume of solution in litres (V)}} \text{ or } C = \frac{n}{V}$$

This equation can be represented in the form of a triangle:

It is important to remember that when using this relationship the volume (**V**) **must** be quoted in **litres** and that **1 litre = 1000 cm³**.

Look out for

To convert a volume from cm³ to litres you divide by 1000.

Example 6: What is the concentration of a solution of hydrochloric acid containing 0.1 mol of hydrogen chloride in 50 cm³ of solution?

You are given the number of moles of solute, **n** = 0.1 mol, and the volume of the solution,

$$V = 50 \text{ cm}^3 = \frac{50}{1000} = 0.05 \text{ litres.}$$

Using the triangle you can work out the concentration of the solution (**C**):

$$C = \frac{n}{V} = \frac{0.1}{0.05} = 2 \text{ mol/l}$$

Example 7: What volume of 2.0 mol/l sodium carbonate solution contains 0.50 mol of sodium carbonate?

You are given the concentration of the solution, **C** = 2.0 mol/l, and the number of moles of solute, **n** = 0.50 mol. Using the triangle you can work out the volume of the solution (**V**):

$$V = \frac{n}{C} = \frac{0.50}{2.0} = 0.25 \text{ litres} = 0.25 \times 1000 = 250 \text{ cm}^3$$

Example 8: How many moles of solute are there in 100 cm³ of 0.4 mol/l sodium hydroxide solution?

You are given the concentration of the solution, **C** = 0.4 mol/l, and the volume of the solution,

$$V = 100 \text{ cm}^3 = \frac{100}{1000} = 0.1 \text{ litres.}$$

Using the triangle you can work out the number of moles of solute (**n**) in the solution:

$$n = C \times V = 0.4 \times 0.1 = 0.04 \text{ mol}$$

Example 9: What mass of potassium nitrate (KNO_3) is required to make 200 cm³ of a 2.50 mol/l potassium nitrate solution?

Since the volume of the solution, **V** = 250 cm³ = 0.250 litres, and the concentration of the solution, **C** = 2.50 mol/l, are known, you can work out the number of moles of potassium nitrate (**n**) needed using the triangle:

$$n = C \times V = 2.50 \times 0.250 = 0.625 \text{ mol}$$

To calculate the mass of potassium nitrate required you need to work out the **GFM,** the mass of one mole, of potassium nitrate:

$KNO_3(s)$ GFM = 39 + 14 + 3(16) = 101 g

1 mol ⟷ 101 g

0.625 mol ⟷ $\frac{0.625}{1} \times 101$

= 63.1 g

continued

What you should know at Credit level – continued

Example 10: What is the concentration of a solution which contains 26.5 g of sodium carbonate (Na_2CO_3) in 500 cm³ of solution?

You first work out the GFM of sodium carbonate and use that to find the number of moles in 26.5 g of the substance.

$Na_2CO_3(s)$ GFM = 2(23) + 12 + 3(16) = 106 g

$$106 \text{ g} \longleftrightarrow 1 \text{ mol}$$

$$26.5 \text{ g} \longleftrightarrow \frac{26.5}{106} \times 1$$

$$= 0.250 \text{ mol}$$

Knowing the number of moles of solute, **n** = 0.250 mol, and the volume of the solution, **V** = 500 cm³ = 0.500 litres, you can work out the concentration of the solution (**C**) using the triangle:

$$\mathbf{C} = \frac{n}{V} = \frac{0.250}{0.500} = 0.50 \text{ mol/l}$$

Credit question 1

The names of some oxides are shown in the grid.

A	B	C
sodium oxide	potassium oxide	copper(II) oxide
D	E	F
carbon dioxide	zinc oxide	sulphur dioxide

Identify the **two** oxides which dissolve in water to form alkaline solutions.

Ⓐ	Ⓑ	C
D	E	F

*Non-metal oxides dissolve in water to form acidic solutions so D and F can be eliminated. Metal oxides will dissolve in water to form alkaline solutions **only** if they are soluble. You need to look up page 5 of the data booklet to find out the solubility of these metal oxides. You will find that copper(II) oxide and zinc oxide are insoluble and so C and E can be eliminated.*

Credit question 2

The grid shows some statements which can be applied to different solutions.

A	It does not conduct electricity.
B	It contains equal numbers of positive and negative ions.
C	Its H^+ ion concentration would increase when water is added.
D	Its concentration of H^+ ions is less that its concentration of OH^- ions.
E	When it is electrolysed, hydrogen gas would be produced at the negative electrode.

Look out for

Insoluble non-metal oxides do **not** dissolve in water and can not form acidic solutions. **Insoluble metal oxides and hydroxides** do **not** dissolve in water and can not form alkaline solutions.

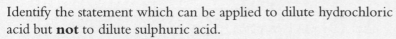

Identify the statement which can be applied to dilute hydrochloric acid but **not** to dilute sulphuric acid.

The answer is B.

One way of doing this is to look at each statement in turn and decide whether it applies only to dilute hydrochloric acid. All acid solutions contain ions and will therefore conduct electricity, A can be ruled out. For B you need to consider the ionic formulae for the two acids. Dilute hydrochloric acid has the formula: $H^+(aq) + Cl^-(aq)$ and dilute sulphuric acid has the formula: $2H^+(aq) + SO_4^{2-}(aq)$. You can see that sulphuric acid contains twice as many positive H^+ ions as negative SO_4^{2-} ions but hydrochloric acid contains equal numbers of positive H^+ ions and negative Cl^- ions. The statement is therefore true for hydrochloric acid

but not for sulphuric acid and so the correct answer is B. Although you've arrived at the correct answer you should check through the remaining statements. When any acid is diluted its pH would increase but its H^+ ion concentration would decrease so C is not a correct answer. D is incorrect as well since in any acid the concentration of H^+ ions is always greater than the concentration of OH^- ions. When any acid is electrolysed the positively charged H^+ ions would be attracted to the negative electrode and converted into hydrogen gas, but E is not a correct answer because the statement applies to both acids and not just hydrochloric acid.

Credit question 3

The graph shows the relationship between the solubility of carbon dioxide in water and the temperature of the water.

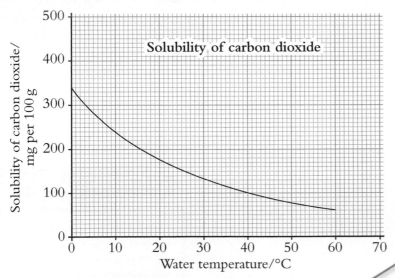

(a) Describe the relationship shown by the graph.

*The solubility of carbon dioxide decreases as the water temperature increases **or** the solubility of carbon dioxide increases as the water temperature decreases.*

*You must be very careful in questions like this to get the relationship the right way round. If you had said 'the water temperature increases as the solubility decreases', you would not have got the mark. It is the change in water temperature that causes the change in solubility and **not** the change in solubility that causes the change in temperature.*

(b) A solution of carbon dioxide is acidic. Explain why the pH will increase when the solution is heated.

When the solution is heated **less carbon dioxide will dissolve in the water and so the solution will become less acidic.** *As a result the pH will increase.*

(c) At 40 °C, 100 mg or 0.100 g of carbon dioxide (CO_2) dissolves in 100 g of water. Calculate the number of moles of carbon dioxide in 0.100 g of carbon dioxide.

$CO2$ $GFM = 12 + 2(16) = 44 g$

$44 g \longleftrightarrow 1 mol$

$0.100 g \longleftrightarrow \dfrac{0.100}{44} \times 1$

$= 0.0023 mol$

You are given the formula for carbon dioxide and so you can work out the gram formula mass (GFM) using the relative atomic masses given on page 4 of the data booklet. The GFM is the mass of one mole and you can then use that to calculate the number of moles in 0.100 g.

Look out for

When calculating gram formula masses make sure that you have correctly worked out the number of each type of atom in the formula. For example, in the compound with formula $(NH_4)_3PO_4$, there are **3** N atoms, **12** H atoms, **1** P atom and **4** O atoms.

Reactions of acids

What you should know at General **level...**

Neutralisers are:

▶ substances which **react with acids** to form water and cancel out the effect of acids.
▶ used in everyday life, for example:

Neutraliser	Use
lime (calcium oxide)	neutralises acid soil and the acidity in lochs caused by acid rain
indigestion tablets	neutralises acids in the stomach
toothpaste	neutralises the acid in plaque

The **reaction between an acid and a neutraliser** is known as a **neutralisation reaction**.

In a neutralisation reaction:

▶ the **pH of the acid moves towards 7.**
▶ the **hydrogen ions of the acid** go to **form water**.

The **three main types** of substances which act as **neutralisers** are:

▶ **alkalis** such as sodium hydroxide solution and potassium hydroxide solution.
▶ **metal oxides** such as calcium oxide and copper oxide.
▶ **metal carbonates** such as sodium carbonate and calcium carbonate.

Examples of an **acid** reacting with an **alkali**:

▶ hydrochloric acid + sodium hydroxide solution → **water** + sodium chloride solution
▶ sulphuric acid + potassium hydroxide solution → **water** + potassium sulphate solution
▶ nitric acid + lithium hydroxide solution → **water** + lithium nitrate solution

In these neutralisation reactions the **pH of the acid moves up towards 7**, the **pH of the alkali moves down towards 7** and **water is always formed**.

Examples of an **acid** reacting with a **metal oxide**:

▶ hydrochloric acid + calcium oxide → **water** + calcium chloride solution
▶ sulphuric acid + copper oxide → **water** + copper sulphate solution
▶ nitric acid + aluminium oxide → **water** + aluminium nitrate solution

Again, **water is always formed** in these neutralisation reactions.

Examples of an **acid** reacting with a **metal carbonate**:

▶ hydrochloric acid + copper carbonate → **water** + **carbon dioxide** + copper chloride solution
▶ sulphuric acid + sodium carbonate → **water** + **carbon dioxide** + sodium sulphate solution
▶ nitric acid + calcium carbonate → **water** + **carbon dioxide** + calcium nitrate solution

You will notice here that, in addition to water, **carbon dioxide gas** is **always formed**.

This type of neutralisation reaction explains why buildings made of limestone (calcium carbonate) and rocks made of carbonates are gradually 'eaten' away by acid rain. It is the hydrogen ions in the acid rain that react with the carbonates.

Metal compounds such as sodium chloride, copper sulphate and calcium nitrate formed in neutralisation reactions are known as **salts**.

continued

Salts formed from:

▶ **hydrochloric acid** are called **chlorides.**
▶ **sulphuric acid** are called **sulphates.**
▶ **nitric acid** are called **nitrates**.

The **neutralisation reactions between an acid and a neutraliser are summarised** in the following table:

Reactants	Products
ACID + ALKALI	→ WATER + SALT
ACID + METAL OXIDE	→ WATER + SALT
ACID + METAL CARBONATE	→ WATER + CARBON DIOXIDE + SALT

Look out for

Acids also react with some metals giving off hydrogen gas. For example:

▶ hydrochloric acid + magnesium → **hydrogen** + magnesium chloride solution
▶ sulphuric acid + zinc → **hydrogen** + zinc sulphate solution

In the reaction of an acid with a metal:

▶ **hydrogen gas** and a **salt** are **always** formed.
▶ the **hydrogen ions** of the acid go to **form hydrogen molecules**.

This type of reaction explains why structures made of iron are gradually 'eaten' away by acid rain. It is the hydrogen ions in the acid rain that react with the iron.

It is important to remember that **not all metals react with acids**. If you look at page 7 of the data booklet it is only those metals above hydrogen in the list that react with acids – those below hydrogen such as copper, silver, mercury and gold do not react with acids.

The **reaction between an acid and a metal** is **not** an example of a neutralisation reaction. The reason for this is that **hydrogen is formed and not water**.

Sometimes when two solutions are added together the reaction mixture turns cloudy. For example:

The cloudiness is caused by the formation of an insoluble solid known as a **precipitate**. If the cloudy solution is left to stand then the precipitate sinks to the bottom of the test tube. It can be separated from the reaction mixture by filtration.

The reaction taking place is:

copper sulphate solution + sodium carbonate solution
↓
cloudy green solution

leave to stand →

colourless solution of sodium sulphate

green precipitate of copper carbonate

copper sulphate solution + sodium carbonate solution → copper carbonate **solid** + sodium sulphate solution

This is an example of a **precipitation reaction** and you can see that the reactants have swapped partners in the formation of the precipitate of copper carbonate.

But how **can you tell if a precipitate is going to form when two solutions are mixed together**? Suppose silver nitrate solution was added to sodium chloride solution. If a reaction took place then silver chloride and sodium nitrate would be formed. If you look up page 5 of the data booklet you find that silver chloride is insoluble and sodium nitrate is soluble. Since silver chloride is insoluble, this means that a precipitation reaction will take place. You **always** have to check the solubilities of the products to find out if a precipitation reaction has taken place.

General question 1

Pupils in a class added different chemicals to dilute hydrochloric acid.

A	B	C
magnesium	magnesium hydroxide	silver

D	E	F
silver carbonate	zinc carbonate	zinc oxide

(a) Identify the chemical which does **not** react with dilute hydrochloric acid.

A	B	Ⓒ
D	E	F

(b) Identify the **two** chemicals which produced **only** a salt and water when reacted with dilute hydrochloric acid.

A	Ⓑ	C
D	E	Ⓕ

Knowing that metal hydroxides (alkalis), metal oxides and metal carbonates neutralise dilute acids, you can eliminate B, D, E and F. Some metals react with acids and these are the ones above hydrogen in the list of metals on page 7 of the data booklet. Magnesium is above hydrogen in this list and silver is below it.

! Look out for

Remember that metals **below** hydrogen in the list on page 7 of the data booklet do **not** react with acids.

*A salt and water are always produced in a neutralisation reaction. The reaction between a metal and a dilute acid is **not** a neutralisation reaction because hydrogen is formed and not water, ruling out A and C. All of the others produce a salt and water when they neutralise a dilute acid, but in the case of silver carbonate and zinc carbonate, carbon dioxide is also formed. B and F are the only two chemicals in the grid that produce **only** a salt and water.*

General question 2

Lorraine added **excess** magnesium carbonate to dilute hydrochloric acid in a beaker.

$$MgCO_3(s) + 2HCl(aq) \rightarrow MgCl_2(aq) + CO_2(g) + H_2O(l)$$

The contents of the beaker were then filtered.

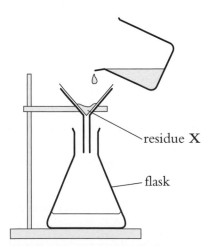

residue **X**

flask

A	magnesium carbonate ($MgCO_3$)	D	carbon dioxide (CO_2)
B	hydrochloric acid (HCl)	E	water (H_2O)
C	magnesium chloride ($MgCl_2$)		

(a) Identify the residue **X**.

The answer is **A**.

(b) Identify the **two** substances which collected in the flask.

The answers are **C** and **E**.

You can see from the diagram that **X** is a solid and the clue to identifying it is the word 'excess'. This means that Lorraine added more than enough magnesium carbonate to neutralise all the acid and so some magnesium carbonate will be left unreacted. If you look at page 5 of the data booklet you will find that magnesium carbonate is insoluble and so will collect in the filter paper. It is good practice to check the other substances just in case. The carbon dioxide is a gas and escapes into the atmosphere and the hydrochloric acid and magnesium chloride are solutions so they would pass through the filter paper as would the water.

A can be eliminated because magnesium carbonate is insoluble and would not pass through the filter paper. B can also be eliminated because all the hydrochloric acid would be used up in the reaction since excess magnesium carbonate was used. Looking at the equation for the reaction you see that magnesium chloride solution, carbon dioxide and water are produced. The carbon dioxide being a gas will escape into the atmosphere but the magnesium chloride solution and the water will pass through the filter paper into the flask.

General question 3

Magnesium sulphate is a compound present in Epsom salts.

(a) Name the elements present in magnesium sulphate.

Magnesium sulphate contains **magnesium, sulphur** and **oxygen**.

It obviously contains magnesium, the 'sulph' part of the name indicates sulphur and the '-ate' ending tells you there is also oxygen.

(b) A solution can be made by dissolving magnesium sulphate in water.
What term can be used to describe the water?

The water is the **solvent**.

A solution is formed when a solute dissolves in a solvent. The magnesium sulphate is the solute.

(c) When drops of barium chloride solution are added to magnesium sulphate solution a solid forms and the mixture turns cloudy.

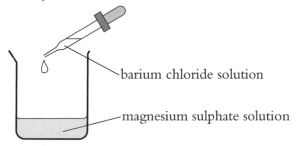

barium chloride solution

magnesium sulphate solution

You are told that a solid forms and this is backed up by the fact that the solution turns cloudy. The solid formed on adding two solutions together can be described as a precipitate.

(i) What type of chemical reaction takes place?

The reaction taking place is a **precipitation** reaction.

(ii) Name the solid formed in this reaction.
You may wish to use page 5 of the data booklet.

The solid formed is barium sulphate.

In a precipitation reaction the two solutions that are added together swap partners. Barium chloride and magnesium sulphate will react to form barium sulphate and magnesium chloride. By looking up page 5 of the data booklet, you find that magnesium chloride is soluble and barium sulphate is insoluble.

General question 4

Chalk (calcium carbonate) is used to give a matt (non-shiny) finish to paper. The more chalk used, the better the matt finish. The mass of chalk used can be found by placing a weighed sample of paper in dilute hydrochloric acid. The chalk reacts and the paper can then be dried and weighed.

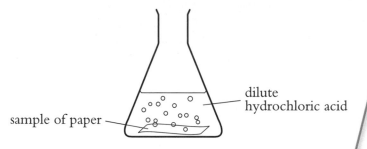

sample of paper

dilute hydrochloric acid

(a) What type of chemical reaction is taking place?

*A **neutralisation** reaction is taking place.*

(b) Name the gas given off during the reaction.

*The gas given off is **carbon dioxide**.*

(c) A class at Robertson High School investigated different types of paper. Here are their results.

	Paper A	Paper B	Paper C	Paper D
Initial mass / g	1.0	1.0	1.0	1.0
Final mass / g	0.7	0.9	0.6	0.8
Loss of mass / g	0.3	0.1	0.4	0.2

Which sample of paper had the best matt finish?

*Paper **C** had the best matt finish.*

You should recognise calcium carbonate as a neutraliser.

Look out for

Make sure you remember that **water and a salt are always formed in a neutralisation reaction**. Carbon dioxide is only formed in the neutralisation reaction between an acid and a carbonate.

The hydrochloric acid reacts with the calcium carbonate in the paper sample to produce carbon dioxide which escapes into the atmosphere. The loss in mass is equal to the mass of carbon dioxide given off and the more carbon dioxide produced the more chalk (calcium carbonate) is in the paper. You are told that the more chalk used the better the matt finish. This means that you are looking for the paper that produced the most carbon dioxide and therefore had the greatest loss in mass.

What you should know at **Credit** **level...**

The neutralisation reactions between acids and neutralisers can be explained by writing ionic formulae equations.

▶ **Acid plus alkali**

Hydrochloric acid for example reacts with sodium hydroxide solution to form water and the salt sodium chloride solution.

$$H^+(aq) + Cl^-(aq) + Na^+(aq) + OH^-(aq) \rightarrow H_2O(l) + Na^+(aq) + Cl^-(aq)$$

You will notice that the Na^+ ions and Cl^- ions don't change during the reaction. They are known as **spectator ions** because they don't take part in the reaction. Rewriting the equation without the spectator ions gives:

$$H^+(aq) + OH^-(aq) \rightarrow H_2O(l)$$

This equation shows that when **any acid** reacts with **any alkali** the only chemical change taking place is the reaction between the **hydrogen ions** (from the acid) and the **hydroxide ions** (from the alkali) to form **water**.

continued

What you should know at Credit level – continued

▶ **Acid plus metal oxide**

Sulphuric acid for example reacts with copper(II) oxide to form water and the salt copper(II) sulphate solution.

$$2H^+(aq) + SO_4^{2-}(aq) + Cu^{2+}O^{2-}(s)$$
$$\downarrow$$
$$H_2O(l) + Cu^{2+}(aq) + SO_4^{2-}(aq)$$

Here the spectator ions are the Cu^{2+} ions and the SO_4^{2-} ions and so the equation for the underlying reaction is: $2H^+(aq) + O^{2-}(s) \rightarrow H_2O(l)$

This equation shows that **any acid** will react with **any metal oxide** to form water.

▶ **Acid plus metal carbonate**

Sulphuric acid for example reacts with sodium carbonate to form water, carbon dioxide and the salt sodium sulphate solution.

$$2H^+(aq) + SO_4^{2-}(aq) + (Na^+)_2CO_3^{2-}(s)$$
$$\downarrow$$
$$H_2O(l) + CO_2(g) + 2Na^+(aq) + SO_4^{2-}(aq)$$

The spectator ions are the Na^+ ions and the SO_4^{2-} ions and the equation for the underlying reaction is:

$$2H^+(aq) + CO_3^{2-}(s) \rightarrow H_2O(l) + CO_2(g)$$

It shows that **any acid** reacts with **any carbonate** to form water and carbon dioxide.

The following table shows the formulae of hydrochloric, nitric and sulphuric acids and the formulae of some of the **salts** made from these acids.

Acid	Salts
H^+Cl^-	Na^+Cl^-, K^+Cl^-, $Ca^{2+}(Cl^-)_2$, $NH_4^+Cl^-$
$H^+NO_3^-$	$Li^+NO_3^-$, $Mg^{2+}(NO_3^-)_2$, $Ca^{2+}(NO_3^-)_2$, $NH_4^+NO_3^-$
$(H^+)_2SO_4^{2-}$	$(Na^+)_2SO_4^{2-}$, $Cu^{2+}SO_4^{2-}$, $Zn^{2+}SO_4^{2-}$, $(NH_4^+)_2SO_4^{2-}$

You can see from the formulae that **a salt is a substance in which the hydrogen ions of an acid have been replaced by metal ions or ammonium ions** (NH_4^+).

A **base is a substance which neutralises an acid**. This means that metal oxides, metal hydroxides and metal carbonates are all examples of bases. Ammonia (NH_3) is also an example of a base.

Those **bases that are soluble form alkalis when added to water**. For example the base sodium oxide is soluble in water and forms the alkali sodium hydroxide solution. The base copper(II) oxide however, is insoluble in water and does not form an alkali when it is added to water.

Look out for

The terms '**base**' and '**alkali**' are often confused. Bases are metal oxides, metal hydroxides, metal carbonates or ammonia. An alkali is the solution that is formed when a **soluble** base is added to water. For example sodium hydroxide is a base and because it is soluble it forms an alkali when dissolved in water. Copper hydroxide is also a base but it could never be classified as an alkali because it is insoluble in water.

Samples of soluble salts can be prepared by **reaction between an acid and**:

▶ **an alkali.**

For example the steps involved in making crystals of **sodium chloride** from hydrochloric acid and sodium hydroxide solution are illustrated below:

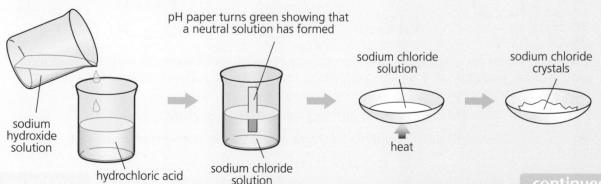

sodium hydroxide solution

pH paper turns green showing that a neutral solution has formed

sodium hydroxide solution

hydrochloric acid

sodium chloride solution

sodium chloride solution

heat

sodium chloride crystals

continued

What you should know at Credit level – continued

Sodium hydroxide solution is added to hydrochloric acid until the solution is neutral. This can be checked using pH paper. The sodium chloride solution is then heated and the water evaporates off leaving crystals of sodium chloride.

▶ **an insoluble metal oxide or an insoluble metal carbonate or a metal.**

As an example the steps involved in making crystals of **copper(II) sulphate** from sulphuric acid and insoluble copper(II) carbonate are illustrated below:

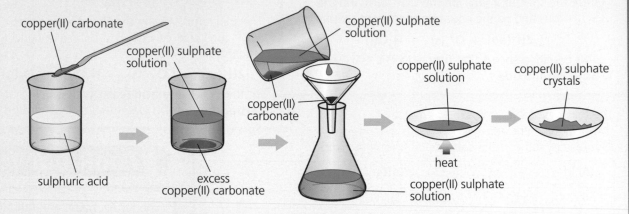

Copper(II) carbonate is added to the sulphuric acid until no more bubbles of carbon dioxide are given off. Excess copper(II) carbonate is used to make sure all the acid reacts and the excess is then removed by filtration. The copper(II) sulphate solution is heated and the water evaporates off leaving crystals of copper(II) sulphate.

The same procedure is used when preparing a salt from an insoluble metal oxide and from a metal.

Samples of insoluble salts can be prepared by **precipitation reactions**. For example the steps involved in making **lead(II) iodide** are illustrated below. Initially solutions of a soluble lead(II) salt such as lead(II) nitrate and a soluble iodide such as potassium iodide are prepared.

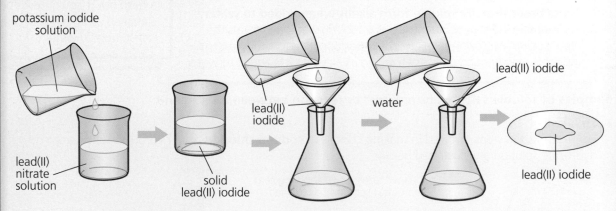

The two solutions are mixed and a yellow precipitate of lead(II) iodide forms. In order to obtain a pure sample of this insoluble salt it is filtered off, washed with water and allowed to dry. The ionic formula equation for the reaction is:

$$Pb^{2+}(NO_3^-)_2(aq) + 2K^+I^-(aq) \rightarrow Pb^{2+}(I^-)_2(s) + 2K^+NO_3^-(aq)$$

The spectator ions are $K^+(aq)$ ions and $NO_3^-(aq)$ ions and so the underlying reaction is:

$$Pb^{2+}(aq) + 2I^-(aq) \rightarrow Pb^{2+}(I^-)_2(s)$$

continued

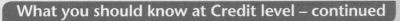

What you should know at Credit level – continued

Titration is an experimental technique which is used to determine the accurate concentration of a solution by reacting it with a solution of known concentration. Suppose you wanted to find the concentration of a solution of sulphuric acid given a 0.25 mol/l sodium hydroxide solution. 25.0 cm³ of the sodium hydroxide solution is measured, by pipette, into a conical flask along with a few drops of indicator. The reading on the burette is recorded and the sulphuric acid is slowly run into the conical flask until the indicator just changes colour. This marks the end–point of the titration. The final burette reading is recorded and from the two burette readings the volume of sulphuric acid needed to exactly neutralise the sodium hydroxide solution can be calculated. The titration is then repeated until at least two volumes are within 0.2 cm³ of each other. The volumes are then said to be concordant.

The table below shows some typical results.

Titration	1	2	3
Initial burette reading / cm³	0.5	19.5	0.3
Final burette reading / cm³	19.5	37.9	18.9
Volume of sulphuric acid used / cm³	19.0	18.4	18.6

The average volume of sulphuric acid required = 18.5 cm³

You will notice that in calculating the average volume the first titration volume is ignored. This is because it is not close enough to the other two values (not concordant) and is a rough titration.

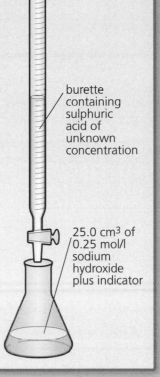

burette containing sulphuric acid of unknown concentration

25.0 cm³ of 0.25 mol/l sodium hydroxide plus indicator

From the results of titration experiments you must be able to work out the concentration of an acid or alkali.

Continuing with the above example, sodium hydroxide reacts with dilute sulphuric acid to form water and sodium sulphate solution:

$$2NaOH(aq) + H_2SO_4(aq) \rightarrow H_2O(l) + Na_2SO_4(aq)$$

In a titration experiment an average of 18.5 cm³ of sulphuric acid was needed to react with 25.0 cm³ of 0.25 mol/l sodium hydroxide solution. Calculate the concentration of the sulphuric acid.

Look out for

In questions based on titrations you are often given results for several titrations. A common error is to calculate the average volume of acid (or alkali) for **all** the titration results. It is **only** those volumes which are close in value (within 0.2 cm³ of each other) that you average.

Method 1: For the sodium hydroxide you are given the volume (V = 25.0 cm³ = 0.0250 litres) and concentration (C = 0.25 mol/l). This allows you to work out the number of moles (n) of sodium hydroxide:

NaOH: $n = C \times V = 0.25 \times 0.0250 = 0.00625$ mol

From the balanced equation you can then work out how many moles of sulphuric acid will react with 0.00625 mol of sodium hydroxide.

$$2NaOH(aq) + H_2SO_4(aq) \rightarrow H_2O(l) + Na_2SO_4(aq)$$

2 mol $\longleftrightarrow$ 1 mol

0.00625 mol $\longleftrightarrow \dfrac{0.00625}{2} \times 1$

$= 0.003125$ mol

Knowing the number of moles of acid (n = 0.003125 mol) and the volume of acid (V = 18.5 cm³ = 0.0185 litres), you can finally calculate the concentration of the acid:

H_2SO_4: $C = \dfrac{n}{V} = \dfrac{0.003125}{0.0185} = 0.169$ mol/l

continued

What you should know at Credit level – continued

Method 2: In this alternative method we use the relationship:

$$P_{acid} \times V_{acid} \times C_{acid} = P_{alkali} \times V_{alkali} \times C_{alkali}$$

where **P** is the power of the acid or alkali

V is the volume of the acid or alkali in cm^3

C is the concentration of the acid or alkali in mol/l

The power of an acid is the number of hydrogen ions in its formula, e.g. hydrochloric acid (HCl) has a power of 1 and sulphuric acid (H_2SO_4) has a power of 2.

The power of an alkali is the number of hydroxide ions in its formula e.g. sodium hydroxide (NaOH) has a power of 1 and calcium hydroxide ($Ca(OH)_2$) has a power of 2.

In our example:

sulphuric acid has **P** = 2, **V** = 18.5 cm^3 and the concentration **C** is unknown,

sodium hydroxide has **P** = 1, **V** = 25.0 cm^3 and **C** = 0.25 mol/l.

On substituting these values in the above relationship, you get:

$$2 \times 18.5 \times C_{acid} = 1 \times 25.0 \times 0.25$$

$$C_{acid} = \frac{1 \times 25.0 \times 0.25}{2 \times 18.5} = 0.169 \text{ mol/l}$$

In this method, the volumes could also be expressed in litres rather than cm^3 and you would arrive at the same answer. In method 1, however, the volumes **must** be in litres.

Credit question 1

The grid shows the names of some chemical compounds.

A sodium hydroxide	B potassium nitrate	C sodium chloride
D lithium carbonate	E sodium phosphate	F barium sulphate

(a) Identify the **two** bases.

Ⓐ	B	C
Ⓓ	E	F

You should remember that bases are substances which neutralise acids and examples of bases include metal oxides, metal hydroxides and metal carbonates, A is a metal hydroxide and D is a metal carbonate.

(b) Identify the compound which could be prepared by precipitation.
   You may wish to refer to page 5 of the data booklet.

A	B	C
D	E	Ⓕ

There are two clues here. One is 'precipitation' which is the reaction used to prepare an insoluble salt. The other is 'page 5 of the data booklet' which shows a table of solubilities. You have to identify which of the above compounds is insoluble. By consulting page 5 you find that barium sulphate is insoluble.

Credit question 2

Identify the **two** results obtained in the reaction between dilute sulphuric acid and barium hydroxide solution.
You may wish to use the data booklet to help you.

A	The pH of the acid went down.
B	Carbon dioxide was produced.
C	A precipitate was formed.
D	Hydrogen was produced.
E	Water was produced.

The answers are **C** and **E**.

A neutralisation reaction takes place when sulphuric acid reacts with barium hydroxide forming water and barium sulphate. Result A can be ruled out because the pH of an acid goes up **not** down when an acid is neutralised. B can also be eliminated because carbon dioxide is only produced when an acid neutralises a carbonate. A precipitate is an insoluble solid and when you look up page 5 of the data booklet you will find that barium sulphate is insoluble. C is a correct answer. In a neutralisation reaction water is always a product but never hydrogen, so D is wrong but E is correct.

Credit question 3

Clare carried out an experiment to make copper chloride crystals.

Instructions for the preparation of copper chloride crystals

Step 1 Add 25 cm^3 of dilute hydrochloric acid to a beaker.

Step 2 Add a spatulaful of copper carbonate powder to the acid and stir.

Step 3 Continue adding copper carbonate until some of the solid remains.

Step 4

Step 5

(a) Why did Clare continue to add copper carbonate until some solid remained.

   Clare did this to make sure that all the acid had reacted with the copper carbonate.

(b) Name the **two** techniques which Clare would have carried out in steps **4** and **5** to prepare a sample of copper chloride crystals.

   Step 4 is **filtration** and step 5 is **evaporation**.

After step 3 the beaker will contain copper chloride solution and unreacted copper carbonate. The copper carbonate needs to be removed from the mixture by filtration. After removing the copper carbonate you are left with copper chloride solution and to get crystals of copper chloride you need to get rid of the water by evaporation.

Look out for

Titration calculations tend to be poorly done in exams. Two methods of approaching these were outlined on pages 74 and 75. You should decide on which one to use and always stick to that method.

Making electricity

What you should know at General **level...**

Batteries or **cells:**

▷ are found in a wide variety of products including mobile phones, cameras, torches, radios, remote controls, laptops, iPods, Mp4 players.
▷ **produce electricity** when **the chemicals in them react together.**
▷ **need to be replaced** or **recharged** when the chemicals in them are used up and the reaction stops.

The **lead–acid battery** used in cars is an example of a **rechargeable battery** and a cutaway diagram of it is illustrated here.

Once the reaction stops and the battery no longer produces electricity, it can be recharged. In the recharging process the chemical reaction is reversed and the chemicals needed to produce electricity in the first place are reformed – electrical energy is converted into chemical energy.

The terms 'battery' and 'cell' are often used to mean the same thing but strictly speaking a device used to produce electricity is a cell, and a battery is a collection of two or more cells linked together. If you look at the diagram above you can see that a lead–acid battery is correctly called a battery because it consists of six cells linked together.

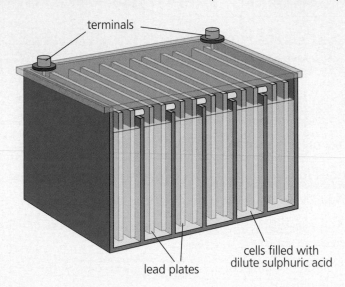

terminals

cells filled with dilute sulphuric acid

lead plates

Batteries have some advantages over **mains electricity,** but there are disadvantages as well:

▷ mains electricity is supplied at 240 V while most batteries produce less than 12 V. Batteries are **safer** as there is virtually no risk of suffering electric shocks.
▷ batteries are **portable**. Appliances which run on them can be used in and out of the home, without the need to plug into the mains.
▷ batteries use up valuable chemicals some of which are finite and will eventually run out. Most mains electricity is generated by burning fossil fuels and these too are finite. However, **less finite resources** are used up by batteries.
▷ battery electricity is **more expensive** than mains electricity.

A **simple cell** like that shown opposite consists of **two different metals** (connected by a piece of wire) dipping into an **electrolyte**. The current of electricity produced in the cell is carried by **electrons** (e^-) from the zinc electrode to the copper electrode through the connecting wires.

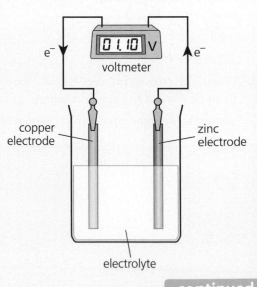

e^- e^-

voltmeter

copper electrode

zinc electrode

electrolyte

continued

What you should know at General level – continued

The **electrolyte** is a solution that contains ions and its purpose is **to complete the circuit**. Ammonium chloride solution is commonly used as an electrolyte. In the lead–acid cell above the electrolyte is dilute sulphuric acid.

When **different pairs of metals** are used in simple cells it is found that they have **different voltages** and this lead to an **electrochemical series** being established.

The electrochemical series can be found on page 7 of the data booklet and it is useful in making predictions about cells:

▶ **electrons will flow** in the connecting wires of a cell **from the metal which is higher in the series to the one that is lower**. For example if you look at page 7 you will see that in a magnesium/silver cell the electrons would flow from magnesium to silver since magnesium is higher in the electrochemical series.

▶ **the further apart the two metals** are in the electrochemical series **the larger is the cell voltage**. For example if you look at page 7 you will see that a magnesium/silver cell would produce a bigger voltage than a magnesium/zinc cell since magnesium and silver are further apart than magnesium and zinc.

Look out for

The **purpose of an electrolyte in a cell** is often forgotten. It is there to complete the circuit – if there was a gap in the circuit then no current of electricity would flow.

Cells like the one shown opposite can also be set up to produce electricity. They are known as **ion-bridge cells** and are made up of two half-cells, each consisting of a piece of metal dipping into a solution containing **ions of the same metal**. These half-cells are connected externally by a piece of wire and internally by an ion-bridge. The **ion-bridge** can be a piece of filter paper soaked in an electrolyte, and is there **to complete the circuit**. In this particular cell electrons flow through the connecting wires from magnesium to copper since magnesium is higher in the electrochemical series.

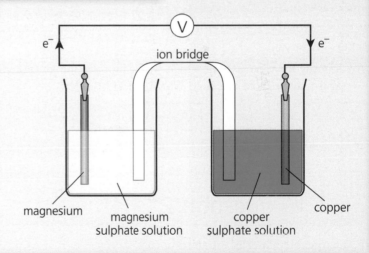

A **displacement reaction** occurs when a **metal is added to a solution containing ions of a metal lower in the electrochemical series**. When a piece of copper is placed in silver nitrate solution for example, the copper becomes coated in silver and the solution turns blue.

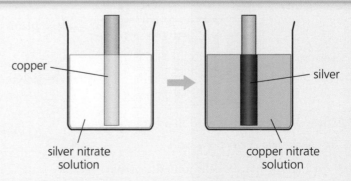

The equation for the reaction is:

copper + silver nitrate solution → copper nitrate solution + silver
(brown)   (colourless)   (blue)   (grey)

The copper is said to have **displaced** the silver from the silver nitrate solution.

General question 1

Electricity can be produced using electrochemical cells.

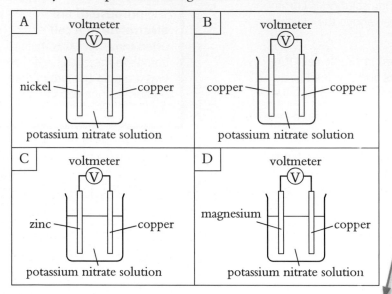

(a) Identify the arrangement which would **not** produce electricity.

A	Ⓑ
C	D

(b) Identify the arrangement which would produce the greatest voltage.
You may wish to use page 7 of the data booklet.

A	B
C	Ⓓ

In B the metals are both copper and so no electricity would be produced.

Look out for

It is important to keep in mind that electricity will be produced in a cell only if two **different** metals are used. If the metals are the same then no reaction takes place and no electricity will be produced.

The electrochemical series is found on page 7 of the data booklet and you will remember that the further apart the metals are in the electrochemical series the greater will be the voltage. Magnesium is further from copper than is nickel or zinc.

General question 2

Rechargeable batteries are used in cars.

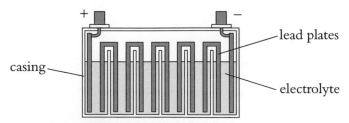

(a) Name the electrolyte used in a car battery.
   <u>The electrolyte is sulphuric acid.</u>

A car battery is also known as a lead–acid battery.

(b) A car battery has six cells joined together.
   The voltage of a car battery is **12 volts**.
   What is the voltage of one of the cells in the car battery?
   <u>One cell has a voltage of 2 volts.</u>

Divide the total voltage by the number of cells to give you the voltage of one cell.

General question 3

The diagram shows a copper/zinc cell.

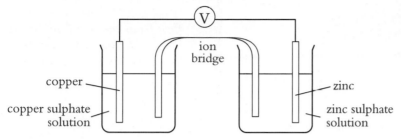

(a) In the cell the electricity flows through the wires from the zinc to the copper.
Name the type of charged particle that flows through the **wires**.

Electrons.

The connecting wires are made of metal which means that the charged particles flowing through them must be electrons.

(b) What is the purpose of the ion-bridge?

An ion-bridge is there to complete the circuit.

(c) Eventually the cell would stop producing electricity.
Give a reason for this.

*In a cell the electricity comes from a chemical reaction. The cell will stop producing electricity **when one of the chemicals is used up** and the reaction can no longer take place.*

(d) Name a metal which could replace zinc to produce a larger voltage.
You may wish to use page 7 of the data booklet to help you.

*The answer is either aluminium **or** magnesium.*

The further apart the metals are in the electrochemical series the larger will be the voltage, so you need a metal higher than zinc in the electrochemical series. If you look at page 7 you will see that aluminium, magnesium, sodium, calcium, potassium and lithium seem to be options. However using sodium, calcium, potassium or lithium would be impractical since they could react violently with the solution.

General question 4

Batteries can be used to power everyday items. A battery is a number of cells joined together.

(a) (i) What happens inside a battery to produce electricity?

*A **chemical reaction** takes place in a battery and produces the electricity.*

(ii) Suggest an advantage in using a battery rather than mains electricity.

*A battery is portable **or** safer than mains electricity.*

(b) A simple cell can be made from everyday objects.

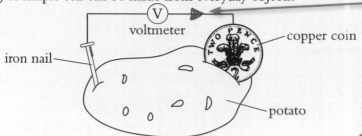

voltmeter

iron nail

copper coin

potato

*If you look at page 7 of the data booklet you will see that iron is above copper in the electrochemical series. Electrons **flow from the metal higher to the one lower in the series**. Notice that the electrons flow through the wires **not** through the potato.*

(i) Draw an arrow **on the wire** to show the direction of electron flow.

(ii) What would happen to the voltage if the iron nail was replaced with aluminium foil? You may wish to use page 7 of the data booklet.

*The voltage would **increase**.*

Aluminium and copper are further apart in the electrochemical series than iron and copper.

Look out for

Consulting the electrochemical series is essential when predicting voltage sizes. Remember that **the further apart the metals are in the series, the larger will be the voltage**.

What you should know at **Credit** **level...**

In the **ion-bridge cell** shown below you already know that electrons would flow from the nickel to the copper since nickel is higher in the electrochemical series. But why does this happen? The position of a metal in the electrochemical series is a measure of how readily it forms ions – the higher it is the more readily it forms ions.

In this cell nickel is the higher metal and so the nickel atoms will form nickel ions:

$$Ni(s) \rightarrow Ni^{2+}(aq) + 2e^-$$

The electrons produced in the process travel through the connecting wires to the copper electrode and join with the copper ions in the copper sulphate solution to form copper atoms:

$$Cu^{2+}(aq) + 2e^- \rightarrow Cu(s)$$

Remember that the **ion-bridge** is there to complete the circuit – it does this by allowing ions to flow from one half–cell to the other.

Ion-bridge cells can also be set up in which one of the half-cells contains a **non-metal** rather than a metal. An example of such a cell is shown opposite in which bromine is the non-metal involved. You can see that the electrons flow from the zinc to the carbon electrode.

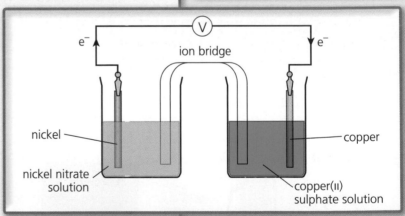

ion bridge

e^- e^-

nickel

copper

nickel nitrate solution

copper(II) sulphate solution

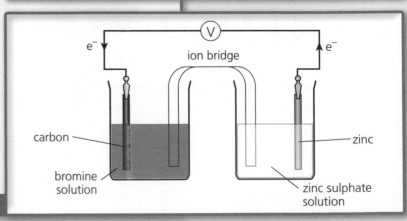

ion bridge

e^- e^-

carbon

zinc

bromine solution

zinc sulphate solution

continued

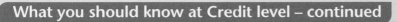

What you should know at Credit level – continued

This means that electrons are being formed at the zinc electrode when the zinc atoms form ions.

$$Zn(s) \rightarrow Zn^{2+}(aq) + 2e^-$$

The electrons travel through the connecting wires to the carbon electrode. There the bromine molecules in the bromine solution gain these electrons and form bromide ions.

$$Br_2(aq) + 2e^- \rightarrow 2Br^-(aq)$$

In a non-metal half-cell, a carbon electrode is used. It does not take part in the reaction but must be there to conduct electrons to or away from the solution in the half-cell.

Displacement reactions can be used to establish the position of hydrogen in the electrochemical series. When **a metal reacts with an acid a displacement reaction takes place**. For example:

$$Mg(s) + 2H^+Cl^-(aq) \rightarrow H_2(g) + Mg^{2+}(Cl^-)_2(aq)$$

The magnesium has displaced the hydrogen from the hydrochloric acid.

Lead and all metals above it in the electrochemical series displace hydrogen from acids but copper and those below do not. This means that **hydrogen occupies a position between lead and copper in the electrochemical series**.

Look out for

The **reaction between a metal and an acid** is often incorrectly described as a neutralisation reaction. Hydrogen not water is produced and so it cannot be a neutralisation reaction. It is of course a **displacement reaction** but it could also be classified as a **redox reaction** since the metal atoms are oxidised and the hydrogen ions of the acid are reduced

Oxidation is a loss of electrons by a reactant in any reaction. For example when a metal reacts to form a compound the metal is said to be **oxidised**. Consider the reaction:

$$2Zn(s) + O_2(g) \rightarrow 2Zn^{2+}O^{2-}(s)$$

The Zn atoms lose electrons when they form Zn^{2+} ions and so undergo an oxidation reaction:

$$Zn(s) \rightarrow Zn^{2+}(s) + 2e^-$$

Reduction is a gain of electrons by a reactant in any reaction. For example when a compound reacts to form a metal, the metal ions in the compound are said to be **reduced**.

Consider the reaction:

$$2Hg^{2+}O^{2-}(s) \rightarrow 2Hg(l) + O_2(g)$$

The Hg^{2+} ions gain electrons when they form Hg atoms and so undergo a reduction reaction:

$$Hg^{2+}(s) + 2e^- \rightarrow Hg(l)$$

OIL RIG is a useful mnemonic to help you remember the definitions of oxidation and reduction:

Oxidation	**R**eduction
Is	**I**s
Loss of electrons	**G**ain of electrons

Oxidation and reduction reactions always occur together and these **red**uction/**ox**idation reactions are known as **redox reactions**.

You will notice that in ion–electron equations representing:

▶ an **oxidation** reaction, the **electrons appear on the product side.**
▶ a **reduction** reaction, the **electrons appear on the reactant side**.

Given an ion–electron equation you must be able to identify it as an oxidation or a reduction. For example:

▶ $Fe^{2+}(aq) \rightarrow Fe^{3+}(aq) + e^-$ would represent an oxidation reaction since the electrons are on the product side of the equation.
▶ $SO_4^{2-}(aq) + 2H^+(aq) + 2e^- \rightarrow SO_3^{2-}(aq) + H_2O(l)$ would represent a reduction reaction since the electrons are on the reactant side of the equation.

Credit question 1

There are many different types of chemical reaction.

A	B	C
reduction	precipitation	displacement
D	E	F
redox	neutralisation	oxidation

Identify the following type of reaction.

$$SO_3^{2-}(aq) + H_2O(l) \rightarrow SO_4^{2-}(aq) + 2H^+(aq) + 2e^-$$

A	B	C
D	E	Ⓕ

The clue here is the presence of electrons in the equation. Only in oxidation and reduction reactions would electrons be part of the equation. In this equation the electrons are on the product side.

Look out for

Oxidation and reduction reactions are often mixed up. Oxidation involves a loss of electrons and these electrons will appear on the product side of the equation. Reduction involves a gain of electrons and these electrons will appear on the reactant side of the equation.

Credit question 2

Roy wanted to show that chemicals can be used to produce an electric current.

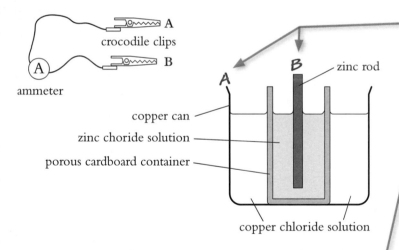

crocodile clips — A, B
ammeter
copper can
zinc choride solution
porous cardboard container
zinc rod
copper chloride solution

You know that the two metals in a cell must be connected if the cell is going to produce electricity. The two metals in this apparatus are the zinc rod and the copper can and so the crocodile clips have to be attached to these. **A** and **B** could be switched round and you would still get the mark.

When the crocodile clips (labelled **A** and **B**) were attached to certain parts of the apparatus the ammeter gave a reading.

(a) Show clearly **on the diagram**, using labels **A** and **B**, where the crocodile clips could have been attached.

(b) Why was no current produced when the porous cardboard container was replaced by a glass beaker?

   *The glass beaker is not porous and so would **not allow the ions** to flow.*

What you have to realise here is that the porous cardboard container is acting as an ion–bridge in the cell and it completes the circuit by allowing ions to flow from one half cell to the other.

(c) What would happen to the reading on the ammeter if the zinc rod was replaced with a tin rod in a tin chloride solution?

   *The reading on the ammeter will be **lower**.*

Using the electrochemical series on page 7 of the data booklet, you will notice that tin is below zinc in the series and so tin and copper are not as far apart as zinc and copper.

Credit question 3

Sarah set up the circuit shown below.

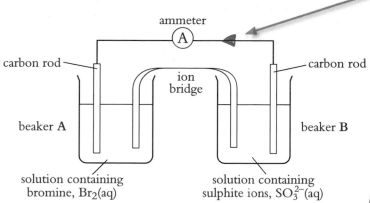

This is a difficult question. You are given the ion–electron equation for the reaction at the carbon rod in beaker **B** and you will notice that it is an oxidation reaction and produces electrons. These electrons will travel through the connecting wires to the carbon rod in beaker **A** where a reduction reaction will take place. The electrons move from the carbon rod in beaker **B** to that in beaker **A**. Remember that electrons flow through metal wires **not** through solutions. Do not put the arrow, indicating electron flow, in the solutions.

In beaker **B** sulphite ions are converted into sulphate ions:

$$SO_3{}^{2-}(aq) + H_2O(l) \rightarrow SO_4{}^{2-}(aq) + 2H^+(aq) + 2e^-$$

(a) On the diagram, clearly mark the path and the direction of the electron flow.

(b) (i) What term is used to describe the type of chemical reaction taking place in beaker B?

It is an **oxidation** reaction.

The electrons appear on the product side of the equation.

(ii) Suggest what would happen to the pH in beaker **B**.

The pH will **decrease**.

Another tricky question. From the equation you can see that $H^+(aq)$ ions are being produced in beaker **B**. This means that the concentration of $H^+(aq)$ ions will increase.

(c) Write the ion–electron equation for the chemical reaction taking place in beaker **A**.
You may wish to use the data booklet to help you.

$Br_2(aq) + 2e^- \rightarrow 2Br^-(aq)$

Since an oxidation reaction takes place in beaker **B** then a reduction reaction must take place in beaker **A** and it must be the bromine molecules (Br_2) that are reduced. You can find the appropriate ion-electron equation on page 7 of the data booklet.

Look out for

Ion–electron equations often lead to a lot of confusion. Remember always to consult page 7 of the data booklet, and take care that you get the equation the correct way round.

Credit question 4

A student added strips of magnesium to solutions of other metals.

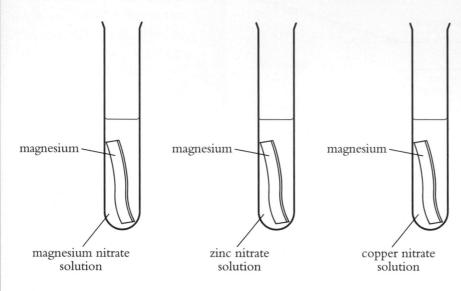

| magnesium | magnesium | magnesium |
| magnesium nitrate solution | zinc nitrate solution | copper nitrate solution |

The results are shown in the table.

Solution / Metal	magnesium nitrate	zinc nitrate	copper nitrate
magnesium	(i) *no reaction*	(ii) *reaction occurred*	reaction occurred

(a) In the table fill in the missing information at (i) and (ii) to show whether or not a chemical reaction has occurred.
You may wish to use the data booklet to help you.

(b) The equation for the reaction between magnesium and copper nitrate is:

$$Mg(s) + Cu^{2+}(aq) + 2NO_3^-(aq) \rightarrow Mg^{2+}(aq) + 2NO_3^-(aq) + Cu(s)$$

(i) Circle the spectator ion in the above equation.

$$Mg(s) + Cu^{2+}(aq) + \boxed{2NO_3^-(aq)} \rightarrow Mg^{2+}(aq) + \boxed{2NO_3^-(aq)} + Cu(s)$$

(ii) What technique could be used to remove the copper from the mixture?

*The copper is in the solid state so it could be removed from the mixture by **filtration**.*

Look out for

It is critical that you remember that **electrons** (not ions) **flow through the connecting wires in a cell** and **ions** (not electrons) **flow through the electrolyte**.

*This question is dealing with displacement reactions. When a metal is added to a solution containing ions of a metal **lower** in the electrochemical series a displacement reaction will take place. By looking up page 7 of the data booklet you find that magnesium is above zinc and so a reaction will take place when magnesium is added to zinc nitrate solution. However nothing will happen when magnesium is added to magnesium nitrate solution.*

Spectator ions do not change in a chemical reaction and if you examine this equation you can see that the NO_3^- ion is the spectator ion. Circling just one of the nitrate ions would gain you the mark as well.

Metals

What you should know at General **level...**

Metals are:

▸ **solids** at room temperature apart from **mercury which is a liquid.**
▸ **conductors of electricity** both in the solid and liquid states – it is their free electrons that allow them to conduct.
▸ **conductors of heat.**
▸ **malleable** – can be beaten into sheets.
▸ **strong.**

Uses of metals depend upon their properties. For example:

▸ **iron** is used to make bridges, buildings, cars, ships and so on because it is very strong.
▸ **aluminium** is used in making aircraft since it has a low density (light) and is strong.
▸ **copper** is used in electrical cables as it conducts electricity well.

Alloys are **mixtures of metals** or **mixtures of metals and non-metals**.

Alloying a metal with another element changes its properties and makes it more suitable for particular uses. For example:

▸ **brass** is an alloy of copper and zinc and is much harder and stronger than either copper or zinc. It is used in musical instruments, plaques and door handles.
▸ **solder** is an alloy of tin and lead and has a lower melting point than tin and lead. This allows it to be used in making electrical connections (soldering).
▸ **'stainless' steel** is used for cutlery and kitchen sinks. It is an alloy of iron, carbon, chromium and nickel. The chromium and nickel prevent the steel rusting.

Some metals react with:

▸ **oxygen** to form **metal oxides**. For example:
$$copper + oxygen \rightarrow copper\ oxide$$
$$2Cu(s) + O_2(g) \rightarrow 2CuO(s)$$
▸ **water** to form **hydrogen and a metal hydroxide**. For example:
$$sodium + water \rightarrow hydrogen + sodium\ hydroxide\ solution$$
$$2Na(s) + H_2O(l) \rightarrow H_2(g) + 2NaOH(aq)$$
▸ **dilute acid** to form **hydrogen and a salt**. For example:
$$magnesium + sulphuric\ acid \rightarrow hydrogen + magnesium\ sulphate\ solution$$
$$Mg(s) + H_2SO_4(aq) \rightarrow H_2(g) + MgSO_4(aq)$$

The speed at which metals react with oxygen, water and dilute acid **gives an indication of the reactivity of the metals – the faster the speed, the more reactive the metal**.

For example, the metals magnesium, copper and zinc can be placed in order of reactivity by observing the speed at which bubbles of hydrogen gas are produced when they are added to dilute sulphuric acid:

The results show that the order of reactivity, starting with the most reactive, is magnesium, zinc then copper.

No bubbles of gas appear in test tube **B** because copper does not react with dilute acid.

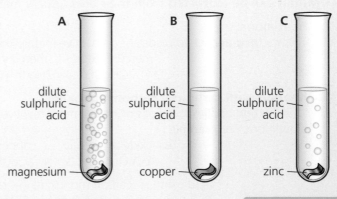

continued

By taking a wide range of metals and observing the speed at which they react with oxygen, water and dilute acid a more complete order of **metal reactivity** can be derived as shown in the following table.

Metal	Reactivity	Reaction with		
		oxygen	water	dilute acid
potassium	most reactive	metal oxide formed	hydrogen and metal hydroxide formed	hydrogen and salt formed
sodium				
lithium				
calcium				
magnesium				
aluminium				
zinc				
iron	decreasing reactivity			
tin			no reaction	
lead				
copper				no reaction
mercury				
silver		no reaction		
gold	least reactive			

The **metal reactivity series** is not given in your data booklet, but if you compare it with the electrochemical series on page 7 you will notice that they are very similar. This means that you can use the electrochemical series as a guide to metal reactivity.

Only a few metals, such as **gold and silver**, are found in the Earth's crust in the **uncombined state**, that is, they are present as metal atoms and not as metal ions. This is because they are so unreactive and it explains why they were among the first metals to be discovered.

The more reactive metals are found in the Earth's crust in the **combined state**, that is, they are present as ions in compounds.

Naturally occurring compounds of metals are known as **ores**.

Metals can be extracted from their ores (usually metal oxides) by:

▸ **heat alone.**
This method applies to oxides of unreactive metals like mercury, silver and gold. For example.
$$\text{mercury oxide} \rightarrow \text{mercury} + \text{oxygen}$$
$$2HgO(s) \rightarrow 2Hg(l) + O_2(g)$$

▸ **heating with carbon or carbon monoxide.**
This method applies to oxides of metals more reactive than mercury but less reactive than aluminium. For example.
$$\text{copper oxide} + \text{carbon} \rightarrow \text{copper} + \text{carbon dioxide}$$
$$2CuO(s) + C(s) \rightarrow 2Cu(s) + CO_2(g)$$

$$\text{lead oxide} + \text{carbon monoxide} \rightarrow \text{lead} + \text{carbon dioxide}$$
$$PbO(s) + CO(g) \rightarrow Pb(s) + CO_2(g)$$

continued

What you should know at General level – continued

Metals that are more reactive than zinc are extracted from their ores by other methods such as electrolysis.

The methods used in extracting metals from their ores are summarised below.

Metal	Method of extraction
potassium sodium lithium calcium magnesium aluminium	**Other methods e.g. electrolysis**
zinc iron tin lead copper	**Heating ore with carbon or carbon monoxide**
mercury silver gold	**Heating ore on its own**

Iron is extracted from iron ore (iron oxide) in a **blast furnace** (see opposite):

The **iron ore** (iron oxide) is loaded in at the top along with **coke** (a form of **carbon**) and limestone.

▶ At **A** the carbon (coke) reacts with the hot air blasted in at the bottom of the furnace to form carbon dioxide.

$$\text{carbon} + \text{oxygen} \rightarrow \text{carbon dioxide}$$
$$C(s) + O_2(g) \rightarrow CO_2(g)$$

▶ At **B** the carbon dioxide reacts with more carbon to form carbon monoxide.

$$\text{carbon dioxide} + \text{carbon} \rightarrow \text{carbon monoxide}$$
$$CO_2(g) + C(s) \rightarrow 2CO(g)$$

▶ At **C** the carbon monoxide reacts with the iron oxide (Fe_2O_3) to form iron and carbon dioxide.

$$\text{iron oxide} + \text{carbon monoxide} \rightarrow \text{iron} + \text{carbon dioxide}$$
$$Fe_2O_3(s) + 3CO(g) \rightarrow 2Fe(l) + 3CO_2(g)$$

The **molten iron** runs down the furnace and collects at the bottom where it is tapped off.

Some metals are **recycled**. One reason for this is that the supply of **metal ores** is limited. They are **finite resources** and will eventually run out.

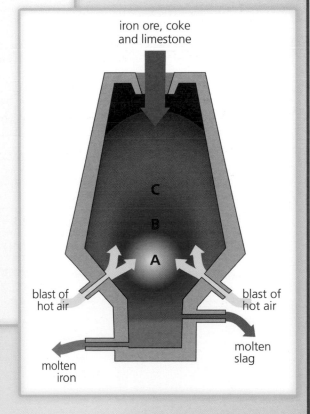

iron ore, coke and limestone

C

B

A

blast of hot air

blast of hot air

molten iron

molten slag

General question 1

The grid shows the names of some metals.

A potassium	B gold	C iron
D zinc	E calcium	F magnesium

(a) Identify the metal found uncombined in the Earth's crust.

A	Ⓑ	C
D	E	F

(b) Identify the metal produced in a blast furnace.

A	B	Ⓒ
D	E	F

(c) Identify the metal which gives a lilac flame colour.
You may wish to use page 4 of the data booklet to help you.

Ⓐ	B	C
D	E	F

If it is uncombined it implies the metal must be very low in the reactivity series. Gold is the most unreactive of these metals.

Look out for

You must learn that iron is produced in a blast furnace. Make sure you **know all the different methods of extracting a metal from its ore**.

On page 4 of the data booklet you will find a table headed 'Flame Colours'. In this table potassium is listed as having a lilac flame colour.

General question 2

Gold and silver are both used to make jewellery.
Identify the **two** statements which are true for **both** gold **and** silver.
You may wish to use the data booklet to help you.

A	They are alkali metals.
B	They conduct electricity.
C	They are more reactive than copper.
D	They react with dilute hydrochloric acid.
E	They are found uncombined in the Earth's crust.

The answers are **B** and **E**.

The alkali metals are in Group I of the Periodic Table. If you look at page I or page 8 of the data booklet you will see that Group I does not include gold or silver, so A can be eliminated. Gold and silver are metals and all metals conduct electricity, therefore B is true. On page 7 of the data booklet you will find that both gold and silver are below copper in the electrochemical series and must be less reactive than copper. C can be eliminated. Also on page 7 you can see both gold and silver are below hydrogen in the electrochemical series and as such, will not react with dilute hydrochloric acid, eliminating D. Gold and silver have a very low reactivity and so can be found uncombined in the Earth's crust.

General question 3

The reactivity of metals can be compared by adding them to a mixture of hydrochloric acid and detergent.
Amy set up five test tubes each containing a different metal.

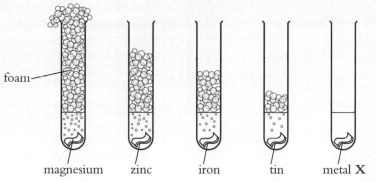

foam

magnesium   zinc   iron   tin   metal **X**

(a) Name the gas produced when a metal reacts with hydrochloric acid.

Hydrogen is the gas produced.

(b) Suggest a name for metal **X**.
You may wish to use page 7 of the data booklet

Metal **X** could be copper, silver or gold.

When a metal reacts with an acid the hydrogen ions (H^+) of the acid go to form hydrogen gas (H_2).

No bubbles of gas are being produced in the test tube containing metal **X**. This means that metal **X** does not react with hydrochloric acid and must be **below** hydrogen in the electrochemical series. By checking the electrochemical series on page 7 of the data booklet you find that metal **X** could be copper, silver, mercury or gold. It is unlikely to be mercury as mercury is a liquid at room temperature and in the diagram metal **X** appears to be a solid piece of metal.

General question 4

Solders are mixtures of lead (melting point 328 °C) and tin (melting point 232 °C).
The graph shows the melting points of solders containing different percentages of tin.

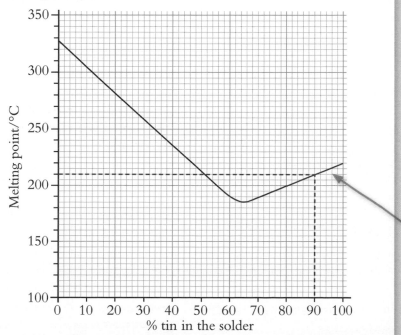

Melting point/°C

% tin in the solder

Look out for

Remember that the speed at which a metal reacts with oxygen, water and dilute acid is a measure of its reactivity – **the faster the reaction speed the more reactive the metal**.

To answer part (c) on page 92, what you have to do is to extend the graph and then read off the melting point when the percentage tin is 90%. The best way to extend the graph is to use a ruler.

(a) What name is given to mixtures of metals like solders?

*Mixtures of metals are called **alloys**.*

(b) Describe the trend in the melting point of solder as the percentage of tin increases from 20% to 50%.

*The melting point of the solder **decreases**.*

(c) Use the graph to estimate the melting point of solder containing 90% tin

The answer is 210 °C.

See previous page.

Look out for

Year after year many candidates incorrectly describe **alloys** as compounds. Make sure you don't make the same mistake. Alloys are **mixtures** of metals or **mixtures** of metals and non-metals. The elements in an alloy are **not** chemically joined.

What you should know at **Credit** level...

When a metal is extracted from its ore **the metal ions in the ore are reduced**.

Consider the extraction of aluminium by electrolysis of its molten oxide (Al_2O_3). The Al^{3+} ions in the aluminium oxide gain electrons and are **reduced** to aluminium atoms:

$$Al^{3+}(l) + 3e^- \rightarrow Al(l)$$

The energy needed to extract a metal from its ore depends on the reactivity of the metal – **the more reactive a metal the more energy is needed to extract it**.

This explains why:

▶ metals more reactive than zinc can **not** be extracted from their metal oxides by heat alone or by heating with carbon or carbon monoxide. These methods do not provide enough energy and so other methods, such as using electricity, have to be employed.
▶ metals in the middle region of the reactivity series (zinc to copper) can **not** be extracted from their metal oxides by heat alone. This method does not provide enough energy and so these metal oxides have to be heated with carbon or carbon monoxide in order to extract the metal.
▶ metals less reactive than copper can be extracted from their metal oxides by heat alone. The heat provides sufficient energy for the reaction to take place.

Given the formula of a compound you must be able to work out the percentage (%) by mass of each element in the compound.

Example 1: Calculate the percentage by mass of each element in sodium nitrate (Na_2CO_3).

$$Na_2CO_3 \text{ GFM} = 2(23) + 12 + 3(16) = 106 \text{ g}$$

$$\% \text{ Na} = \frac{2(23)}{106} \times 100 = 43.4 \%$$

$$\% \text{ C} = \frac{12}{106} \times 100 = 11.3 \%$$

$$\% \text{ O} = \frac{3(16)}{106} \times 100 = 45.3 \%$$

The **empirical formula** of a compound shows the simplest whole number ratio of atoms in that compound. For example the empirical formula of sodium carbonate is Na_2CO_3 and shows that the Na:C:O ratio is 2:1:3.

Given the mass of each element in a compound you must be able to work out its empirical formula.

continued

What you should know at Credit level – continued

Example 2: A sample of copper chloride contained 6.4 g of copper and 7.1 g of chlorine.
Calculate the empirical formula of copper chloride.

One way of doing this is to draw up a table and then follow the steps outlined below:

Step 1. Write down the symbol for each element.

Step 2. Write down the mass of each element.

Step 3. Work out the number of moles of each element by dividing its mass by its relative atomic mass.

Step 4. To get the mole ratio divide the number of moles of each by the smaller of the two.

Element	Cu	Cl
Mass / g	6.4	7.1
Number of moles	$\frac{6.4}{63.5} = 0.10$	$\frac{7.1}{35.5} = 0.20$
Mole ratio	$\frac{0.10}{0.10} = 1$	$\frac{0.20}{0.10} = 2$

There are two chlorines for every one copper so the empirical formula is **$CuCl_2$**.

Given the percentage composition of a compound you must be able to work out its empirical formula.

Example 3: Calculate the empirical formula of the compound that contains 32.4 % sodium, 22.5 % sulphur and 45.1 % oxygen.

If you consider 100 g of the compound then the mass of each element will correspond to its percentage. You then proceed in exactly the same way as above.

Element	Na	S	O
Mass / g	32.4	22.5	45.1
Number of moles	$\frac{32.4}{23} = 1.41$	$\frac{22.5}{32} = 0.70$	$\frac{45.1}{16} = 2.82$
Mole ratio	$\frac{1.41}{0.70} = 2$	$\frac{0.70}{0.70} = 1$	$\frac{2.82}{0.70} = 4$

The empirical formula is Na_2SO_4

You must be able to work out the mass of a reactant or product in a reaction given the balanced equation for the reaction.

Example 4: Methane burns in oxygen to produce carbon dioxide and water:
$$CH_4(g) + 2O_2(g) \rightarrow CO_2(g) + 2H_2O(l)$$
Calculate the mass of water produced on burning 2.7 g of methane.

Step 1. Write the balanced equation for the reaction.

Step 2. Pick out the substances for which a mass is given (methane) and for which a mass has to be found (water) and write down the number of moles of each.

Step 3. Convert the moles into masses.

Step 4. Finally work out the mass of water formed.

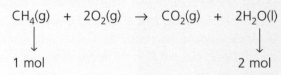

$$CH_4(g) + 2O_2(g) \rightarrow CO_2(g) + 2H_2O(l)$$

1 mol → 2 mol

$12+4(1) = 16$ g ←→ $2[2(1)+16] = 36$ g

2.7 g ←→ $\frac{2.7}{16} \times 36$

$= 6.1$ g

Credit question 1

Daniel is studying the reactions of some metals and their compounds.

He carried out experiments involving magnesium, copper, zinc, nickel, silver and an unknown metal **X**.

Listed below are some of the observations he recorded.

A	**X** was more readily oxidised than copper.
B	**X** oxide was more stable to heat than silver oxide.
C	Magnesium displaced **X** from a solution of **X** nitrate.
D	**X** reacted more vigorously than nickel with dilute acid.
E	The ore of **X** was more readily reduced than the ore of zinc.
F	Compounds of **X** were more readily reduced than compounds of zinc.

From his observations, Daniel produced the following order of reactivity.

magnesium, zinc, nickel, copper, **X**, silver

⟶

decreasing activity

Identify the **two** observations which can be used to show that **X** has been wrongly placed.

The answers are **A** and **D**.

This is a complicated question and there is a lot to work out. You should take each statement in turn.

A – If **X** is more readily oxidised than copper then **X** must be more reactive than copper. This means Daniel has put **X** in the wrong place – it should have been placed before copper. A is one of the answers you are looking for.

B – If **X** oxide is more stable to heat than silver oxide then this implies that **X** must be more reactive than silver. In relation to silver Daniel has placed **X** correctly.

C – If magnesium displaces **X** from a solution of **X** nitrate then magnesium must be more reactive than **X** as Daniel has correctly stated. Remember that a displacement reaction will only occur if a metal is added to a solution containing ions of a metal **lower** in the electrochemical series.

D – If **X** reacted more vigorously than nickel with dilute acid then this means that **X** is more reactive than nickel. Daniel has put **X** in the wrong place – it should have come before nickel. D is the other answer you are looking for.

E – If the ore of **X** was more readily reduced than the ore of zinc then this implies that **X** must be less reactive than zinc. Daniel is correct in placing **X** after zinc.

F – By saying that **X** could be extracted by heating its oxide with carbon implies that it cannot be extracted by heat alone. You know that silver can be extracted by just heating silver oxide and so **X** must be more reactive than silver. Daniel has correctly placed **X** before silver.

Credit question 2

Anglesite is an ore containing lead(II) sulphate, $PbSO_4$.

(a) Calculate the percentage by mass of lead in lead(II) sulphate.

$PbSO_4$ GFM = 207 + 32 + 4(16) = 303 g

% Pb = $\frac{207}{303}$ x 100 = 68.3%

Apply the method described on page 92.

(b) Most metals are found combined in the Earth's crust and have to be extracted from their ores.

Place the following metals in the correct space in the table.

lead   aluminium

You may wish to use the data booklet to help you.

Metal	Method of extraction
aluminium	electrolysis of molten compound
lead	using heat and carbon

From the electrochemical series on page 7 of the data booklet you find that aluminium is a much more reactive metal than lead. This means that it will take much more energy to extract aluminium from its ore than to extract lead from its ore. Using electricity will supply sufficient energy to extract aluminium from its ore but using heat and carbon would not.

Look out for

Calculations always seem to present a lot of difficulties in exam questions. You should learn the methods outlined on pages 92 and 93 and practise them often.

Look out for

It is difficult to get to grips with **the relationship between the reactivity of a metal and the stability of its compounds (or ores)**. If a metal is reactive then its compounds will be very stable and it will require a lot of energy to extract the metal from them. If a metal is unreactive then its compounds will be unstable and it will require very little energy to extract the metal from them.

(c) When a metal is extracted from its ore metal ions are changed into metal atoms.

Name this **type** of chemical reaction.

The reaction taking place is reduction.

Look out for

The **extraction of a metal from its ore** is often incorrectly described as an oxidation reaction. It is a **reduction reaction** because the metal ions in the ore are **gaining** electrons when they are converted into metal atoms.

Credit question 3

Molten iron is used to join steel railway lines together.
Molten iron is produced when aluminium reacts with iron oxide.
The equation for the reaction is:

$$2Al + Fe_2O_3 \rightarrow 2Fe + Al_2O_3$$

Apply the method outlined on page 93.

(a) Calculate the mass of iron produced from 40 g of iron oxide.

$$2Al \quad + \quad Fe_2O_3 \quad \rightarrow \quad 2Fe \quad + \quad Al_2O_3$$

| | I mol | | 2 mol | |

$$2(56) + 3(16) = \qquad\qquad 2(56) =$$

$$160\,g \quad \longleftrightarrow \quad 112\,g$$

$$40\,g \quad \longleftrightarrow \quad \frac{40}{160} \times 112$$

$$= \textbf{28}\,\textbf{g}$$

(b) Iron can also be produced from iron ore, Fe_2O_3, in a blast furnace.

iron ore, coke and limestone

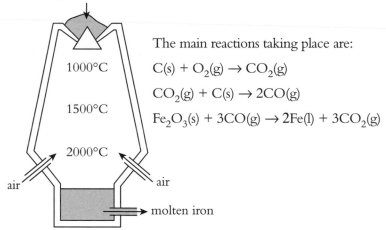

1000°C

1500°C

2000°C

air   air

molten iron

The main reactions taking place are:

$$C(s) + O_2(g) \rightarrow CO_2(g)$$

$$CO_2(g) + C(s) \rightarrow 2CO(g)$$

$$Fe_2O_3(s) + 3CO(g) \rightarrow 2Fe(l) + 3CO_2(g)$$

One of the main reactions in the blast furnace is that between carbon and oxygen to produce carbon dioxide. Air contains the oxygen.

(i) When air is blown into the furnace the temperature rises. Suggest another reason why **air** is blown into the furnace.

*Air is blown into the furnace to provide the **oxygen** needed to react with the carbon.*

(ii) Explain why the temperature at the bottom of the blast furnace should **not** drop below 1535 °C.
You may wish to use the data booklet to help you.

The iron would be in the solid state and would not flow down the furnace.

Looking at the diagram you can see the iron must be in the **molten** state to allow it to flow down the furnace and be tapped off at the bottom. You need to look up page 3 of the data booklet to find the melting point of iron. It is 1535 °C. If the temperature fell below 1535 °C the iron would become solid.

Corrosion

What you should know at General **level...**

Corrosion:

▶ is a reaction on the surface of a metal which involves the metal changing from an element to a compound. The atoms of the metal are changed into ions by losing electrons and the appearance of the metal changes. For example when copper corrodes the copper atoms change into copper ions:

$$Cu \rightarrow Cu^{2+} + 2e^-$$

You can see this change on copper roofs. The brown colour of the copper changes to green.

▶ will affect different metals at different rates. Reactive metals like magnesium corrode quite quickly but unreactive metals like silver are only affected very slowly.

Rusting is a form of corrosion and:

▶ is a term applied to the corrosion of iron and steel only.
▶ needs both oxygen (from the air) and water to take place.
▶ changes iron atoms into Fe^{2+} ions by the loss of two electrons:

$$Fe \rightarrow Fe^{2+} + 2e^-$$

When iron rusts, the appearance of the metal changes. Rust is often a red–brown colour but can also be black.
▶ can be detected by **ferroxyl indicator**. **Ferroxyl indicator** is a yellow colour. It only turns **blue** when $Fe^{2+}(aq)$ ions are present. The more intense the blue colour the greater is the degree of rusting.
▶ is speeded up by the presence of **electrolytes** like salt solution. Car bodies rust more quickly in winter when salt is spread on the roads to make the ice melt.
▶ when iron rusts it loses its strength. Metal objects made of iron would no longer be able to do their job if they get too rusty.

Look out for

Be careful with the use of the word rust. Many metals **corrode** but only iron and steel **rust**. Remember also that iron is an element but steel is an alloy. Steel is a **mixture** of iron and carbon.

Rusting can be **prevented** by:

▶ connecting the iron to a metal higher than iron in the electrochemical series. This is known as **sacrificial protection**. The more reactive metal corrodes and the electrons flow **from** it **to the iron** and so prevents rusting.

Pipelines are protected by sacrificial protection. Scrap magnesium is connected to the pipeline and the magnesium is sacrificed to protect the iron. The magnesium atoms corrode to form magnesium ions and electrons:

$$Mg \rightarrow Mg^{2+} + 2e^-$$

The electrons flow to the iron pipeline and prevent rusting. The scrap magnesium has to be replaced at regular intervals.

▶ connecting the iron to the **negative** terminal of a battery. This supplies the iron with electrons and prevents the iron rusting. Cars have the negative terminal of their battery attached to the body of the car to help prevent rusting.
▶ using a barrier which stops air and water from reaching the surface of the metal. This is known as **physical protection**. The choice of barrier will depend on the use of the iron.

continued

Barrier methods	Coating with	Advantage	Disadvantage	Example
painting	paint	colourful	easily chipped	cars
greasing	grease/wax	cheap	messy	bicycle chains
electroplating	another metal	stays shiny	expensive	handlebars
galvanising	zinc	long lasting	dull appearance	trash cans
tin-plating	tin	stays shiny	expensive	tin cans
coating with plastic	plastic	easy to clean	melts easily	fridge shelves

Galvanising means **coating with zinc**. Articles that need to be galvanised can be dipped into a bath of molten zinc or the zinc can be applied by **electroplating** as shown below.

At the positive electrode the zinc atoms become zinc ions:

$$Zn \rightarrow Zn^{2+} + 2e^-$$

The positive zinc ions are attracted to the negative terminal and are changed back to atoms by gaining two electrons:

$$Zn^{2+} + 2e^- \rightarrow Zn$$

The zinc forms a coating on the iron. Buckets, fences and motorway crash barriers are all examples of galvanised steel.

Galvanised iron is initially protected because the layer of zinc acts as a barrier to oxygen and water. When the layer of zinc is **broken** the zinc also acts sacrificially to protect the iron. This happens because zinc is higher up the electrochemical series than iron. Electrons flow from the **zinc to the iron** and prevent rusting.

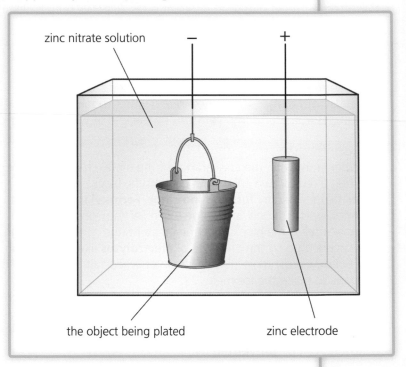

zinc nitrate solution

the object being plated   zinc electrode

Tin coating. Initially the tin coating acts as a barrier to oxygen and water. Iron is above tin in the electrochemical series so when the tin coating is broken electrons **flow from the iron** to the **tin**. The iron corrodes to protect the tin and **rusting is speeded up.**

Look out for

When **electroplating**, the object to be plated must be the **negative** electrode in the plating cell. Many different metals are used in electroplating. The **positive** electrode has to be the metal being used as the plating. The electrolyte should be a solution of a **salt of the metal being used as the plating.** For example to plate an object with nickel, the object will be the negative electrode, the **positive** electrode will be made of nickel and the electrolyte will be a solution of a **nickel salt**.

General question 1

The grid shows the names of some metals.

A	B	C
tin	steel	iron
D	E	F
magnesium	zinc	brass

(a) Identify the two metals which will give a blue colour with ferroxyl indicator.

A	Ⓑ	Ⓒ
D	E	F

(b) Identify the metal used in galvanising steel.

A	B	C
D	Ⓔ	F

(c) Identify the two metals which can be used in the sacrificial protection of steel.

A	B	C
Ⓓ	Ⓔ	F

(d) Identify the two alloys.

A	Ⓑ	C
D	E	Ⓕ

The two alloys are brass and steel. Remember that steel is a mixture of iron and carbon so is an alloy. You could look at the Periodic Table and see which metals from the grid are not listed there but this would take some time. Better to learn the names of a few common alloys – see chapter 11.

Ferroxyl indicator turns blue with Fe^{2+}(aq) ions. Both iron and steel will produce this change.

Look out for

You can show that iron and steel rust by testing with ferroxyl indicator. If you put a piece of iron and steel into ferroxyl indicator both will turn the ferroxyl indicator blue. The speed of rusting can be increased by adding an electrolyte like salt solution. Make sure you always state the colour change, a positive test makes the **yellow** ferroxyl indicator turn **blue.**

Galvanise means to coat with zinc. This is a common question.

You can check the data booklet p7 and see that both magnesium and zinc are above iron in the electrochemical series so will sacrificially protect iron. You could be asked about other metals which could be used to protect iron. These would also have to be higher up the electrochemical series than iron.

Look out for

Sacrificial protection only works with a metal **above** iron in the **electrochemical series** to provide the iron with electrons. Magnesium is often used for sacrificial protection.

General question 2

James set up a series of experiments to investigate the corrosion of iron.

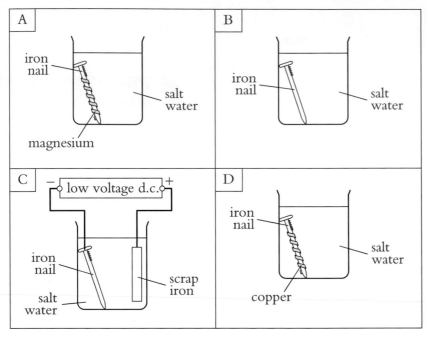

(a) Identify the experiment in which the corrosion of the **nail** was the most rapid.

(b) Identify the experiment in which the iron was sacrificially protected.

A	B
C	D

Taking each box in turn you should see that:
A – the nail is being sacrificially protected by the magnesium so corrosion will be very slow.
B – the iron will corrode. Keep this in mind as you look at the other possible answers.
C – the nail is being prevented from corroding because it is connected to the negative terminal of the power supply.
*D – the nail is connected to copper and is also in a solution of salt which is an electrolyte. Copper is below iron in the electrochemical series. (Any metal below iron in the series could be used in a similar way to speed up the corrosion of iron.) Corrosion here will be **much more rapid** than in B.*

*Magnesium is higher than iron in the electrochemical series so will protect the nail. **Electrons** will flow from the magnesium to the iron to prevent the iron from rusting.*

General question 3

Linda was investigating corrosion. She set up four test tubes each containing a clean nail.

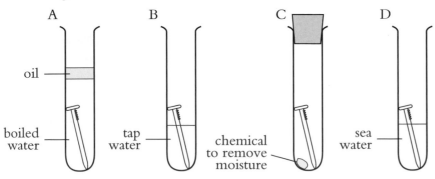

Tube	Observations after 1 week
A	Nail still bright
B	Nail rusted
C	Nail still bright
D	Nail badly rusted

(a) Suggest why the nail in tube A did not rust.

*Rusting needs both oxygen (air) and water. The boiled water has **no dissolved oxygen** left in it and the layer of oil stops more air dissolving in the water. No oxygen means the iron cannot rust.*

(b) Why did the nail in sea water rust more than the nail in tap water?

*Sea water contains dissolved salt. Salt is an **electrolyte and so corrosion is speeded up**.*

(c) Linda added ferroxyl indicator to the tube that contained seawater. The ferroxyl indicator changed colour.

  (i) What colour **change** would Linda see?

  *Ferroxyl indicator is **yellow** and will turn **blue** when added to the tube with the rusty nail.*

When you are asked for a colour *change* you have to give both the **initial** and **final** colours.

  (ii) Write the symbol for the ion that caused the colour change in the ferroxyl indicator.

  *Ferroxyl indicator changes colour with the **Fe^{2+} (aq)** ion.*

You need to learn this.

General question 4

Maureen set up the experiment shown in Diagram **A**. She noticed that the water stopped rising in the test tube when **one fifth** of the air had been used up as shown in Diagram **B**.

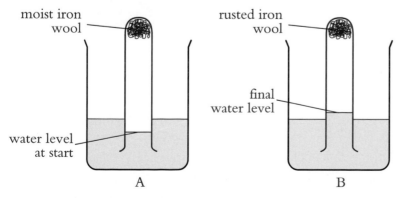

(a) Which gas in air is used up during rusting?

Oxygen is used up during rusting.

The clue is in the diagram. Rusting needs both oxygen (air) and water. Air is approximately one fifth **oxygen**.

(b) Maureen set up another tube using a larger piece of moist iron wool.

How would the final water level compare with that in B?

It would be at the same level.

(c) Write the formula for the iron ion formed during rusting.

_$Fe^{2+}(aq)$_

As all of the oxygen had been used up in B the bigger piece of moist iron wool would cause the water to rise to the same level. It would probably reach this level quicker than the first experiment but that is not the question.

When iron rusts it initially forms the $Fe^{2+}(aq)$ ion. This ion can then go on to form the $Fe^{3+}(aq)$ ion so either formula would be acceptable.

Look out for

▶ The use of the word rust. Many metals corrode but only iron and steel _rust_. Remember also that iron is an element but steel is an alloy. Steel is a _mixture_ of iron and carbon. You can show that iron and steel rust by testing with ferroxyl indicator. If you put a piece of iron and steel into ferroxyl indicator both will turn the ferroxyl indicator blue. You could speed up rusting by adding an electrolyte like salt solution.
▶ The colour change when ferroxyl indicator is used to test for rusting. A positive test makes the yellow ferroxyl indicator turn _blue_.
▶ Sacrificial protection uses a metal _above_ iron in the electrochemical series to provide the iron with electrons. Magnesium is often used for sacrificial protection. With galvanised iron, the zinc coating is initially used as a barrier method of protection. The zinc only acts sacrificially _after the coating_ is _broken_.
▶ Batteries being used to prevent corrosion. Iron has to be connected to the _negative_ terminal of the battery to prevent corrosion.
▶ You should make sure that you learn that galvanising means coating with zinc.

What you should know at **Credit** **level...**

Rusting:

▶ is an example of oxidation. The iron atoms initially form Fe^{2+} ions by losing two electrons:

$$Fe(s) \rightarrow Fe^{2+}(aq) + 2e^-$$

▶ needs **water, oxygen** and an **electrolyte** for it to occur. The electrolyte could be a salt solution or dissolved carbon dioxide or acid rain.
▶ initially forms Fe^{2+} ions which can be further oxidised to Fe^{3+} ions.
▶ produces hydroxide ions since the electrons lost by the iron are gained by the oxygen and water:

$$2H_2O(l) + O_2(g) + 4e^- \rightarrow 4OH^-(aq)$$

This equation can be found on page 7 of the data booklet.

Hydroxide ions turn ferroxyl indicator **pink**.

▶ is an electrochemical process and can be used to set up a cell. Electrons will flow from iron to carbon in a cell. The direction of electron flow can be shown by using ferroxyl indicator.

Look out for

Remember that rusting (corrosion) is an oxidation reaction. You should learn the equation for iron rusting, and for the further oxidation to Fe^{3+}:

$Fe(s) \rightarrow Fe^{2+}(aq) + 2 e^-$

During rusting the iron(II) ions are further oxidised to iron(III) ions

$Fe^{2+}(aq) \rightarrow Fe^{3+}(aq) + e^-$

Credit question 1

Ships can have hulls made from iron. Iron should be protected from rusting.
Identify the correct statement.

A	Rusting is slowed by adding salt to the water.
B	Nickel will give sacrificial protection to iron.
C	Iron rusts faster when connected to the negative terminal of a battery.
D	The rusting of iron is an example of reduction.
E	Ferroxyl indicator turns pink in the presence of $Fe^{2+}(aq)$ ions.
F	Galvanised iron does not even when the coating is scratched.

The answer is **F**.

You will need to look at each statement in turn. Even although you may think you have got the one correct answer it is always better to check all of the statements.

A Salt water **speeds up** rusting. ✗

B Check p7 of data booklet. Nickel is **below** iron in the electrochemical series and so cannot give sacrificial protection. ✗

C Iron connected to the negative terminal is **slowed down in rusting**. ✗

D The rusting of iron is an example of **oxidation**. ✗

E Ferroxyl indicator turns **blue** with $Fe^{2+}(aq)$ ions. It turns **pink** with OH^-. ✗

F Galvanised iron **does not rust** even when the coating is scratched. ✓
The zinc provides sacrificial protection since zinc is above iron in the electrochemical series.

Credit question 2

Iron rusts in the presence of water and oxygen. Electrolytes like sodium chloride speed up the rate of rusting.
The **table** shows a number of chemical equations.

A	$Fe^{3+}(aq) + e^- \rightarrow Fe^{2+}(aq)$
B	$H_2(g) \rightarrow 2H^+(aq) + 2e^-$
C	$2H_2O(l) + O_2(g) + 4e^- \rightarrow 4OH^-(aq)$
D	$NaCl(s) + H_2O(l) \rightarrow Na^+(aq) + Cl^-(aq)$
E	$Fe(s) \rightarrow Fe^{2+}(aq) + 2e^-$
F	$H^+(aq) + OH^-(aq) \rightarrow H_2O(l)$

Identify the **two** equations for the reactions involved in rusting.

The answers are **C** and **E**.

A shows the reduction of iron. Rusting is an oxidation process. ✗

B shows the ionisation of hydrogen and plays no part in rusting. ✗

C shows the production of hydroxide ions and **is** one of the reactions in rusting. ✓

D shows the dissolving of salt and is not part of the reactions in rusting. ✗

E shows the initial step in rusting and **is** one of the reactions in rusting. Note that the iron(II) ions can then oxidise further to iron(III) ions but this reaction is not shown in the table. ✓

F shows the equation for neutralisation. ✗

Credit question 3

The diagram shows how an on object made of iron can be coated with chromium. Chromium lies between iron and zinc in the electrochemical series.

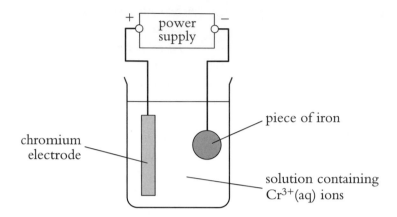

(a) What name is given to this process?

This is an example of **electroplating**.

(b) Write the equation for the reaction that takes place at the iron electrode.

$Cr^{3+}(aq) + 3e^- \rightarrow Cr(s)$

> The iron is being coated with chromium. The $Cr^{3+}(aq)$ ions must be being changed into atoms and the negative electrode supplies the electrons. You will need to add three electrons to balance out the charge on the chromium ions.

(c) **Explain** what will happen to the mass of the chromium electrode during this process.

*The chromium electrode **loses mass as the chromium atoms are converted to ions in solution**.*

> You need to realise that the chromium electrode is being used up in this reaction. It will not be enough to say that the electrode loses mass as this is not an explanation. You need to add that **chromium atoms are converted to ions in solution**. Or you could say that the chromium is being oxidised and being converted from atoms to ions and so is losing mass.

(d) If the chromium coated on the piece of iron is scratched, the iron continues to be protected from rusting.
Give a reason for this.

The chromium protects the iron sacrificially since chromium is above iron in the electrochemical series and supplies electrons to the iron.

> Look at page 7 of the data booklet. Although chromium is not listed there you are told in the introduction to the question that chromium lies between iron and zinc in the electrochemical series. This means that chromium is above iron in the electrochemical series and **will provide sacrificial protection**.

Credit question 4

The cell below was set up.

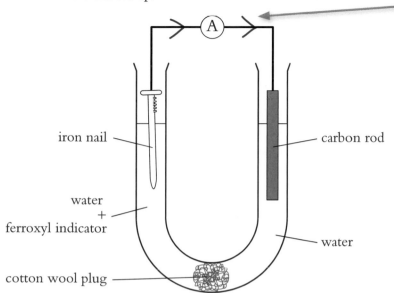

After some time the iron nail had rusted and the ferroxyl indicator had turned blue.

(a) On the diagram mark the path and direction of the electron flow.

You need to show that the electrons will flow from the iron to the carbon through the ammeter. You can do this by drawing arrows on the wires.

(b) What could be added to the water to speed up the rate of rusting?

*An **electrolyte** could be added to the water e.g. **sodium chloride**.*

(c) The reaction taking place at the carbon rod produces hydroxide ions.

   (i) Write the equation for the production of the hydroxide ions.

   The reaction that produces the hydroxide ions is:

   $$2H_2O + O_2 + 4e^- \rightarrow 4OH^-$$

   You should not try to memorise this equation but you do need to remember that you can find it on p7 of the data booklet. If you have tried to memorise, it is always advisable to check that you have got it correct.

   (ii) What could be added to the water surrounding the carbon rod that could be used to show that hydroxide ions were present?

   Ferroxyl indicator could be added which would turn pink with hydroxide ions.

   *You need to think about indicators here. You could add either **universal indicator** which turns purple with hydroxide ions or **ferroxyl indicator** which would turn pink with hydroxide ions. Remember that when you give a test for an answer you must also say what will happen or what you will see.*

Plastics and synthetic fibres

What you should know at General **level...**

Plastics are **synthetic** materials because they are manufactured by the chemical industry and do not occur naturally.

Synthetic fibres are thread–like and they are formed when plastics are melted and squeezed through tiny holes.

Most plastics and synthetic fibres are made from crude oil.

Plastics

- are **strong**
- have a low density, i.e. they are **light**
- are good **electrical** and **heat insulators**
- are resistant to most chemicals which makes them **durable**, i.e. long-lasting.

These properties allow plastics to be used in a variety of ways:

Plastic	Use	Property
polythene	carrier bags, plastic bottles	strong and light
PVC	guttering, window frames	strong and rigid
	covering on electrical cables	electrical insulator
polystyrene	radio and TV casings	hard and rigid
nylon	tooth brush bristles, clothing	strong, hard-wearing and flexible
perspex	motor cycle windshields, solar panels	transparent, hard and shatterproof

Plastics are often used as replacements for **natural materials**. For example:

- PVC is replacing wood in window frames. PVC frames are often cheaper to manufacture and do not need to be painted.
- PVC is also used in place of rubber to insulate electrical cables. PVC does not become brittle whereas rubber does.
- Clothes can be made from the synthetic fibre, polyester. This material is lighter than the natural material cotton and does not crease as easily.

Plastics have **disadvantages** in that they:

- are mostly **non–biodegradable** and this causes environmental problems. If plastics are sent to land fill they take a long time to break down. Natural materials such as wood, paper and food waste are **biodegradable**, i.e. they are broken down by bacteria and eventually rot away.
- generally **burn or smoulder** to give off **toxic fumes**.
- can be made from oil, e.g. PVC, a non–renewable resource. Natural substances such as wood and rubber come from renewable sources.

Plastics can be classed as:

- **thermoplastic** – a thermoplastic softens on heating and so can be melted and reshaped. Polythene, nylon and PVC are all examples of thermoplastics.
- **thermosetting** – a thermosetting plastic does **not** soften on heating and so it **cannot** be melted and reshaped. Kettles and electrical plugs can be made from thermosetting plastics such as a urea–methanal plastic. It is not affected by heat.

continued

What you should know at General level – continued

The raw material used to make plastics and synthetic fibres is crude oil. The crude oil is separated into fractions at the oil refinery. Some of these fractions are then **cracked** to produce alkenes which are unsaturated, i.e. contain a carbon-to-carbon double bond. These alkenes are used as **monomers**, single reactive molecules, to make long-chain molecules called **polymers** in a process called **polymerisation**.

For example ethene monomers join together to form poly(ethene) or polythene as it is more commonly called.

$$\underset{H}{\overset{H}{C}} = \underset{H}{\overset{H}{C}} + \underset{H}{\overset{H}{C}} = \underset{H}{\overset{H}{C}} + \underset{H}{\overset{H}{C}} = \underset{H}{\overset{H}{C}} \rightarrow -\underset{H}{\overset{H}{C}} - \underset{H}{\overset{H}{C}} - \underset{H}{\overset{H}{C}} - \underset{H}{\overset{H}{C}} - \underset{H}{\overset{H}{C}} - \underset{H}{\overset{H}{C}} -$$

This is only *part* of a chain. The bond at each end of the fragment *must* be shown.

  ethene monomers   part of a polythene polymer

The monomers add on to one another so this is called **addition polymerisation** and the polythene formed is an example of an **addition polymer**.

Other examples of addition polymers and the monomers from which they are made are shown in the table below.

Monomer	Polymer
propene	poly(propene)
styrene / phenylethene	polystyrene / poly(phenylethene)
vinyl chloride / chloroethene	poly(vinyl chloride) or PVC / poly(chloroethene)

Plastics and synthetic fibres are examples of polymers. So too are natural fibres like cotton, silk and linen.

Look out for

Monomers used in addition polymerisation **must** contain a carbon-to-carbon double bond. Alkanes **cannot** form polymers. Learn the names of the monomers used to make addition polymers. Monomers must be unsaturated so their names will end in **ene**. For example polypropene is made from propene.

General question 1

The grid shows the names of some types of chemical terms.

A addition	B cracking	C oxidation
D reduction	E combustion	F polymerisation

(a) Identify the term which describes the production of small, unsaturated molecules used to make plastics.

  The term used to describe this process is cracking.

(b) Identify the two terms which can be used in the reaction:

  ethene → polythene

Ⓐ	B	C
D	E	Ⓕ

You need to know the meaning of **all** of the terms in the grid. They do not all come from this topic. The term you are looking for here is cracking. (See chapter 6 if you need to remind yourself about cracking.)

You need to know that polymers, like polythene, are made in a process of **polymerisation** (F). Most polymers whose name ends in **ene** will be made from an alkene. Alkenes form **addition** (A) polymers.

General question 2

Some cars have their bumpers, boot lids and bonnets made out of plastic rather than steel.

(a) Suggest an advantage in using plastic rather than steel.

One advantage of using plastic is that it is lighter than steel.

(b) Plastics are synthetic.
What is meant by the term **synthetic**?

Synthetic means **man made**.

(c) Why are the fumes from burning plastics dangerous?

The fumes are **toxic** or **poisonous**.

There are a number of acceptable answers here. You could say that **plastic is lighter** or you could say that **plastic will not rust**. Remember that you have to say which is lighter. It is not enough to write 'it is lighter' as you are not explaining what 'it' is.

General question 3

Polythene is an addition polymer made from monomers called ethene.

(a) Draw a section of polythene showing three monomer units joined together.

$$
\begin{array}{c}
\overset{\displaystyle H}{\underset{\displaystyle H}{C}} = \overset{\displaystyle H}{\underset{\displaystyle H}{C}} \;+\; \overset{\displaystyle H}{\underset{\displaystyle H}{C}} = \overset{\displaystyle H}{\underset{\displaystyle H}{C}} \;+\; \overset{\displaystyle H}{\underset{\displaystyle H}{C}} = \overset{\displaystyle H}{\underset{\displaystyle H}{C}} \quad\rightarrow\quad -C-C-C-C-C-C-
\end{array}
$$

(b) Polythene cannot be used for making pot handles as it softens and changes shape when heated.
What term is used to describe a polymer that changes shape on heating?

Polythene is a **thermoplastic**.

(c) One of the major problems with the use of polythene is how to dispose of it. Polythene is not biodegradeable.
What is meant by biodegradeable?

Something which is biodegradeable will **break down** or **rot**
**naturally** by the action of bacteria and fungi. **Or** you could say
**break down naturally** by the action of microorganisms.

The best way to answer this question is to draw the six carbon atoms with **single** bonds between them. Then add the hydrogen atoms. You need to make sure that there are 4 **bonds on each carbon**. Remember to include the bonds on the end carbon atoms. You could if you wish put the section in brackets with a subscript n after it.

$$
\left(-C-C-C-C-C-C- \right)_n
$$

Look out for

A common mistake is to forget the **two bonds** on the end carbons. As this is only **part** of the polymer chain the end two carbons must **not** have hydrogen atoms on them.

Make sure that you know the difference between **thermoplastic** and **thermosetting**.

What you should know at Credit level...

In addition polymerisation unsaturated monomers join together by first opening up the carbon-to-carbon double bond. Consider for example the formation of poly(propene) from its monomer propene (C_3H_6).

$$H - \overset{\overset{\displaystyle H}{|}}{\underset{\underset{\displaystyle H}{|}}{C}} - \overset{}{\underset{\underset{\displaystyle H}{|}}{C}} = \overset{}{\underset{\underset{\displaystyle H}{|}}{C}} - H$$

Draw the monomer units in the shape of the letter H with the double bond horizontal:

$$\underset{\underset{\displaystyle H}{|}}{\overset{\overset{\displaystyle H}{|}}{C}} = \underset{\underset{\displaystyle CH_3}{|}}{\overset{\overset{\displaystyle H}{|}}{C}} \qquad \underset{\underset{\displaystyle H}{|}}{\overset{\overset{\displaystyle H}{|}}{C}} = \underset{\underset{\displaystyle CH_3}{|}}{\overset{\overset{\displaystyle H}{|}}{C}} \qquad \underset{\underset{\displaystyle H}{|}}{\overset{\overset{\displaystyle H}{|}}{C}} = \underset{\underset{\displaystyle CH_3}{|}}{\overset{\overset{\displaystyle H}{|}}{C}}$$

Then open up the double bonds:

$$- \underset{\underset{\displaystyle H}{|}}{\overset{\overset{\displaystyle H}{|}}{C}} - \underset{\underset{\displaystyle CH_3}{|}}{\overset{\overset{\displaystyle H}{|}}{C}} - \qquad - \underset{\underset{\displaystyle CH_3}{|}}{\overset{\overset{\displaystyle H}{|}}{C}} - \underset{}{\overset{\overset{\displaystyle H}{|}}{C}} - \qquad - \underset{\underset{\displaystyle CH_3}{|}}{\overset{\overset{\displaystyle H}{|}}{C}} - \overset{\overset{\displaystyle H}{|}}{C} -$$

Then link up the bonds between the carbon atoms making sure that there is an open bond showing on the end carbon atoms:

$$- \overset{\overset{\displaystyle H}{|}}{\underset{\underset{\displaystyle H}{|}}{C}} - \overset{\overset{\displaystyle H}{|}}{\underset{\underset{\displaystyle CH_3}{|}}{C}} - \overset{\overset{\displaystyle H}{|}}{\underset{\underset{\displaystyle H}{|}}{C}} - \overset{\overset{\displaystyle H}{|}}{\underset{\underset{\displaystyle CH_3}{|}}{C}} - \overset{\overset{\displaystyle H}{|}}{\underset{\underset{\displaystyle H}{|}}{C}} - \overset{\overset{\displaystyle H}{|}}{\underset{\underset{\displaystyle CH_3}{|}}{C}} -$$

Polymer chains are made up of **repeating** units. The repeating unit is the smallest part of a chain that can be added to copies of itself to make up the polymer chain. Given the structure of a polymer, you must be able to identify the repeating unit and draw its structure. You must also be able to draw the structure of the monomer from which it was made. Consider PVC which has the following structure:

$$- \overset{\overset{\displaystyle Cl}{|}}{\underset{\underset{\displaystyle H}{|}}{C}} - \overset{\overset{\displaystyle H}{|}}{\underset{\underset{\displaystyle H}{|}}{C}} - \overset{\overset{\displaystyle Cl}{|}}{\underset{\underset{\displaystyle H}{|}}{C}} - \overset{\overset{\displaystyle H}{|}}{\underset{\underset{\displaystyle H}{|}}{C}} - \overset{\overset{\displaystyle Cl}{|}}{\underset{\underset{\displaystyle H}{|}}{C}} - \overset{\overset{\displaystyle H}{|}}{\underset{\underset{\displaystyle H}{|}}{C}} -$$

The repeating unit in PVC is:

$$- \overset{\overset{\displaystyle Cl}{|}}{\underset{\underset{\displaystyle H}{|}}{C}} - \overset{\overset{\displaystyle H}{|}}{\underset{\underset{\displaystyle H}{|}}{C}} -$$

If you remake the double bond between the two carbon atoms you will form the structure of the monomer used to make PVC:

$$\overset{\overset{\displaystyle Cl}{|}}{\underset{\underset{\displaystyle H}{|}}{C}} = \overset{\overset{\displaystyle H}{|}}{\underset{\underset{\displaystyle H}{|}}{C}}$$

The toxic gases given off when plastics burn depends on the elements present.

Name of plastic	Use	Elements present in plastic	Toxic gases produced on burning in air
polythene	plastic bags	C,H	Carbon monoxide, CO
polyvinyl chloride	double glazed window frames	C,H,Cl	Carbon monoxide, CO Hydrogen chloride, HCl
polyurethane	foam cushions foam mattresses	C,H,N,O.	Carbon monoxide, CO hydrogen cyanide, HCN

Any plastic which contains carbon can produce the toxic gas carbon monoxide if it burns in a limited supply of air. PVC contains hydrogen and chlorine so can produce toxic fumes of hydrogen chloride (HCl). Polyurethane is a polymer used in foam cushions and mattresses. This polymer contains carbon, nitrogen and hydrogen. These elements can produce the very toxic gas hydrogen cyanide (HCN) during combustion.

Credit question 1

The structure below shows part of a polymer molecule used as a glue.

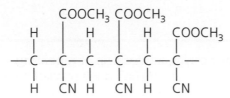

The grid shows the names of some gases.

A	B	C
CH$_4$	CO$_2$	HCN

D	E	F
CO	HCl	H$_2$

Identify the **two** poisonous gases which may be produced when this polymer burns.

A	B	Ⓒ
Ⓓ	E	F

There are two things you need to remember here. The gas has to be poisonous and the elements of the gas have to be present in the polymer. Take each box in turn:

A Methane is not poisonous ✗
B Carbon dioxide is not poisonous ✗
C HCN hydrogen cyanide is poisonous and all three elements are present in the polymer. ✓
D Carbon monoxide is poisonous and can be caused by burning any carbon containing material in a limited supply of air. ✓
E HCl is poisonous but there is no chlorine in the polymer used to make the glue. HCl cannot be formed here. ✗
F Hydrogen is not poisonous and hydrogen burns to produce water. ✗

Credit question 2

Polybutene is a plastic made from butene C$_4$H$_{10}$. Butene has the structure:

(a) What name is given to the reaction which converts butene to polybutene?

The reaction is called addition polymerisation.

(b) Draw a section of this polymer showing at least three monomer units joined together.

Butene contains a carbon to carbon double bond so this is an example of **addition polymerisation**. You will need both words to gain the mark for this question.

The first thing to do is draw out the three monomers in an H shape. Make sure that you see where the C2H5- comes from.

It is a good idea to do this in pencil as it makes it easy to make changes. Then remove the double bond and give each carbon 4 bonds.

Now link up the bonds between the carbon atoms. Make sure that the end carbon atoms have an open bond showing that the polymer chain continues.

Credit question 3

Polystyrene is a commonly used plastic. The structure of part of a polystyrene molecule is shown below.

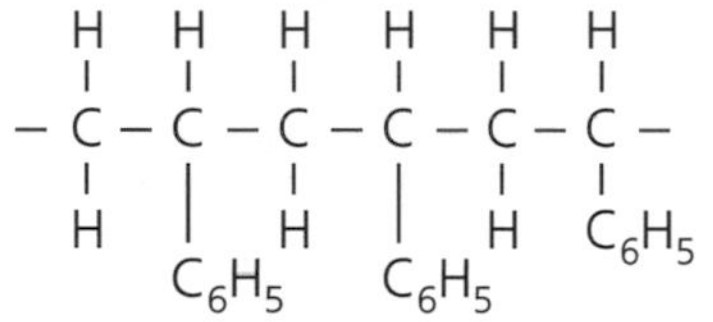

$$
\begin{array}{cccccc}
H & H & H & H & H & H \\
| & | & | & | & | & | \\
-C- & C- & C- & C- & C- & C- \\
| & | & | & | & | & | \\
H & | & H & | & H & C_6H_5 \\
& C_6H_5 & & C_6H_5 & &
\end{array}
$$

(a) Identify the repeating unit in polystyrene.

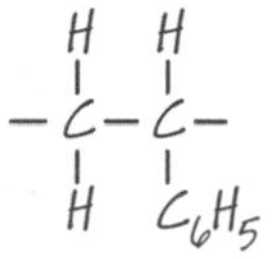

$$
\begin{array}{cc}
H & H \\
| & | \\
-C- & C- \\
| & | \\
H & C_6H_5
\end{array}
$$

The repeating unit is the **smallest** part of the polymer chain that can be added to copies of itself to make the chain.

Once you have found the repeating unit you have to close the double bond. Note if you are asked to draw a structural formula for a monomer from the structure of a polymer you still have to identify the repeating unit.

(b) Draw a structural formula for the monomer from which polystyrene is made.

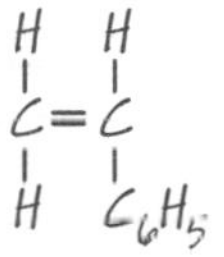

$$
\begin{array}{cc}
H & H \\
| & | \\
C= & C \\
| & | \\
H & C_6H_5
\end{array}
$$

(c) Name a toxic gas that can be produced by burning polystyrene.

Carbon monoxide.

Polystyrene contains only carbon and hydrogen so the toxic gas it can produce on burning is **carbon monoxide**. Polystyrene will also produce carbon dioxide and water during burning but neither of these is toxic.

(d) Give a use for polystyrene and a reason why polystyrene is a suitable material for this use.

Polystyrene is used for foam **cups** to hold hot liquids. When turned into foam, polystyrene is a **good heat insulator**.

There are other uses you could choose such as packaging, just make sure the reason you give **matches** the use you have chosen.

Look out for

Practice identifying repeating units and the monomers used to make a polymer. The repeating unit of the polymer in question 1 above is:

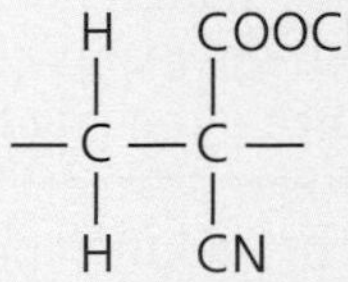

$$
\begin{array}{cc}
H & COOCH_3 \\
| & | \\
-C- & C- \\
| & | \\
H & CN
\end{array}
$$

You should then be able to write the structure for the monomer by reforming the double bond:

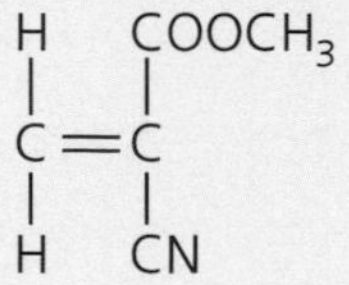

$$
\begin{array}{cc}
H & COOCH_3 \\
| & | \\
C= & C \\
| & | \\
H & CN
\end{array}
$$

Fertilisers

All of our food relies on the growth of plants. With an increasing world population the efficient production of food crops is important. Plants need nutrients including compounds of nitrogen (N), phosphorus (P) and potassium (K). Growing plants remove these nutrients from the soil.

These nutrienrts can be replaced:

▶ naturally by the use of compost or animal manure.
▶ by the use of artificial fertilisers. Ammonium salts (N), nitrates (N), phosphates (P) and potassium salts (K) are all used as artificial fertilisers to restore soil fertility.

The choice of artificial fertiliser will depend not only on the nutrients needed but also on the type of soil, the type of plants being grown and the weather conditions. Plants take up nutrients through their roots so fertilisers have to be soluble. Very soluble fertilisers can be washed out of the soil into rivers and lochs. This excess supply of nutrients can lead to problems such as algal blooms which cut off the oxygen supply to fish and other animals. An excess of nitrate in drinking water causes an increase in stomach cancer in humans. Fertilisers with lower solubility are used in areas of wet ground and places with high rainfall to reduce the amount of nutrient washed away.

Many plants need high levels of the nutrient nitrogen. About 80% of the earth's atmosphere is nitrogen gas. This is referred to as **'free' nitrogen**. Nitrogen is a not a very reactive gas. It takes a lot of energy to convert this 'free' nitrogen into nitrogen compounds that contain **'fixed' nitrogen**.

There are two naturally occurring processes that fix nitrogen.

▶ During lightning storms the high–energy spark allows atmospheric nitrogen to combine with oxygen to make nitrogen dioxide. This dissolves in rain to make a very dilute solution of nitric acid.

$$4NO_2(g) + 2H_2O(l) + O_2(g) \rightarrow 4HNO_3(aq)$$

This **acid rain** replaces nitrogen in the soil but also increases soil acidity. A similar reaction occurs in car engines. (See page 29) Sparking air is not an economical method of producing nitric acid because it takes too much energy.

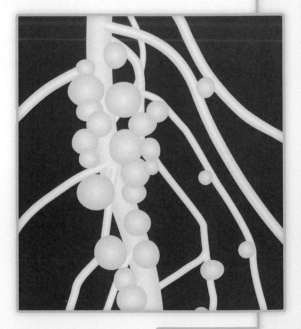

▶ Plants like peas, beans and clover have naturally occurring **nitrogen–fixing bacteria** living in root nodules. These bacteria convert the element nitrogen from the air into fixed nitrogen which the plants can use. The bacteria do not need any extra source of energy to do this so it is a cheaper source of fixed nitrogen than artificial fertilisers. Farmers can plant these crops and then dig them into the soil as a way of raising the level of fixed nitrogen available to other plants.

continued

What you should know at General level – continued

Nitrogen is lost from soil when plants are cropped and transported away. The **nitrogen cycle** shows the recycling of nitrogen from plant and animal remains. It also shows how nitrogen is gained and lost. Modern sewage systems break the cycle by allowing fixed nitrogen to enter the oceans. Artificial fertilisers are needed to replace this loss.

The nitrogen cycle

nitrogen in the **air**

denitrifying bacteria

nitrogen-fixing bacteria in certain plants

nitrogen compounds in **plant** and **animal remains** → bacteria → nitrates and ammonium salts in **soil** → nitrogen in **plant protein**

plants die

eaten by animals

death or excretion

nitrogen in **animal protein**

human waste to the **sea**

At room temperature **ammonia** (NH_3) is a clear, colourless gas with a very distinct, fishy smell. It is extremely soluble in water producing an alkaline solution. This can be shown in the laboratory by the fountain experiment.

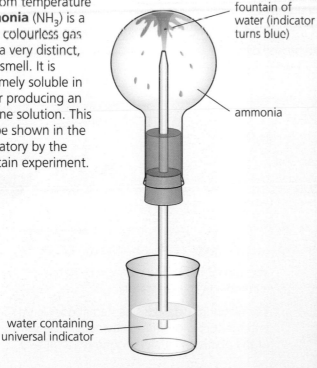

fountain of water (indicator turns blue)

ammonia

water containing universal indicator

Ammonia reacts with acids to produce **ammonium** salts. Ammonium salts contain the ammonium (NH_4^+) ion. Ammonium nitrate which is used as a fertiliser is produced when ammonia reacts with nitric acid.

$$NH_3(g) + H^+NO_3^-(aq) \rightarrow NH_4^+NO_3^-(aq)$$

The industrial production of ammonium nitrate fertiliser needs large quantities of both ammonia and nitric acid.

Different acids can be used to produce different salts of ammonia:

▶ Hydrochloric acid produces ammonium chloride.

▶ Sulphuric acid produces ammonium sulphate.

▶ Phosphoric acid produces ammonium phosphate.

continued

Look out for

Learn the properties of ammonia particularly that it is an alkaline gas. You can test for this with either pH paper (the paper must be **moist**) or universal indicator. Both will turn blue with ammonia.

The Haber process

Ammonia is produced by the **Haber process**.

$$N_2 + 3H_2 \rightleftharpoons 2NH_3$$

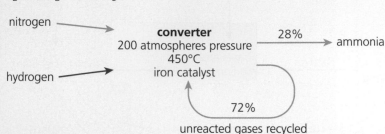

nitrogen ⟶

converter
200 atmospheres pressure
450°C
iron catalyst

28% ⟶ ammonia

hydrogen ⟶

72%

unreacted gases recycled

Nitrogen is extracted from the air. Hydrogen is produced by reacting steam with methane. The nitrogen and hydrogen are **compressed** to a pressure of 200 atmospheres and passed over an **iron** catalyst at about 450 °C. This choice of temperature and pressure gives a reasonable yield without the reaction being too slow. Not all the nitrogen and hydrogen react. The unreacted gases are recycled. The ammonia is cooled to a liquid and removed.

Ammonia is oxidised to nitric acid by the **Ostwald** process. This is a two-stage process.

In the first stage ammonia is mixed with air and passed over a **heated** platinum catalyst.

The following reaction takes place.

ammonia + oxygen → nitrogen dioxide + water

$$4NH_3(g) + 7O_2(g) \rightarrow 4NO_2(g) + 6H_2O(l)$$

The nitrogen dioxide is then mixed with more air and dissolved in water.

nitrogen dioxide + oxygen + water → nitric acid

$$4NO_2(g) + O_2(g) + 2H_2O(l) \rightarrow 4HNO_3(aq)$$

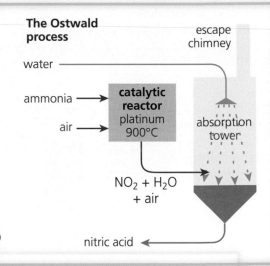

The Ostwald process

water ⟶

ammonia ⟶

air ⟶

catalytic reactor
platinum
900°C

escape chimney

absorption tower

$NO_2 + H_2O$ + air

nitric acid ⟵

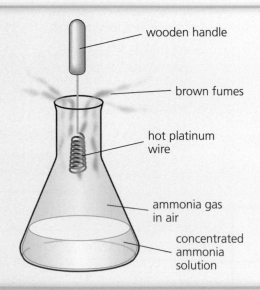

wooden handle

brown fumes

hot platinum wire

ammonia gas in air

concentrated ammonia solution

You can carry out the catalytic oxidation of ammonia in the laboratory.

The platinum catalyst is heated and lowered into the fumes of ammonia and air. The spiral of the platinum catalyst continues to glow.

General question 1

The grid shows the names of some gases.

A	B	C
methane	nitrogen	ammonia
D	E	F
oxygen	carbon dioxide	nitrogen dioxide

(a) Identify the gas which turns moist pH paper blue.

A	B	Ⓒ
D	E	F

Ammonia is the only alkaline gas. This will turn moist pH paper blue or blue/purple.

(b) Identify the two gases which combine in the atmosphere during lightning storms.

A	Ⓑ	C
Ⓓ	E	F

*You should know that the atmosphere contains **nitrogen** and **oxygen**. These two gases do not readily combine but the high-energy spark in lightning allows them to combine.*

General question 2

The table shows the names of some metals.

A	B	C
iron	cobalt	platinum
D	E	F
steel	zinc	tin

(a) Identify the metal used as a catalyst in the Haber process.

Ⓐ	B	C
D	E	F

*You need to learn that **iron** is used as the catalyst in the Haber process.*

(b) Identify the metal used as the catalyst in the Ostwald process.

A	B	Ⓒ
D	E	F

You are unlikely to get both of these questions in one examination paper but you need to be prepared to answer either.

Look out for

Know the names of both industrial processes in this topic, i.e. the Haber process and the Ostwald process. Make sure you are clear about which catalyst is used in each and the conditions used in the process.

General question 3

The Manufacture of Ammonia

The gases nitrogen and hydrogen are mixed together then compressed before passing into a catalyst chamber. Within the catalyst chamber there is an iron catalyst at 500 °C. In the cooler, the ammonia is separated from the unreacted gases. The unreacted gases are recycled.

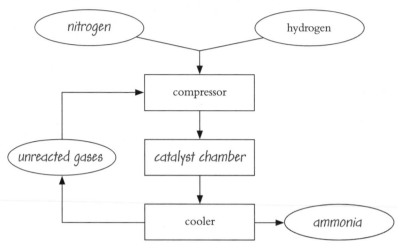

(a) Use the above information to complete the flow chart.

(b) Name the industrial process used to manufacture ammonia.

The Haber process.

(c) Ammonia is reacted with sulphuric acid to make the artificial fertiliser ammonium sulphate.
Write the formula for the ammonium ion.

_NH_4^+ is the formula for the ammonium ion._

In questions like this all the information you need should be in the question. You need to read it carefully.

*You need to learn the name **Haber** process. Think about this name anytime you see a question about ammonia.*

*It is a common mistake to mix up ammonia, NH_3, and ammonium, NH_4^+. Ammonia is a covalent gas. The ammonium **ion** is found in ionic substances. The formula for the ammonium ion is given in the data booklet p4. Do not guess! Look it up. Make sure you **include** the **positive** charge.*

Questions about the Ostwald process or the Haber process often appear in exam papers.

General question 4

The flow diagram shows how ammonia is converted to nitric acid.

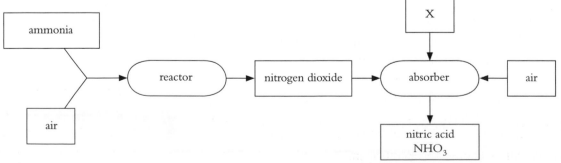

(a) (i) Name the industrial process used to manufacture nitric acid.

Nitric acid is manufactured using the **Ostwald** process.

(ii) Name substance X.

Substance X is **water**.

(b) Name the salt produced by reacting ammonia with nitric acid.

Ammonium nitrate.

Here you have to watch that the name ammonia becomes **ammonium** when it forms a salt. The salts of nitric acid are called nitrates.

Looking at the diagram you will see that nitrogen dioxide and air are being added to the absorber. Both of these only contain the elements nitrogen and oxygen. The product from the absorber is nitric acid. This contains the element hydrogen therefore substance X must contain hydrogen. You should know that nitrogen dioxide is absorbed by **water** when making nitric acid.

What you should know at **Credit** level...

Ammonia can be prepared in the laboratory by heating any ammonium salt with any alkali.

If solid ammonium chloride is heated with sodium hydroxide solution the equation for reaction is:

$NH_4^+Cl^-(s) + Na^+OH^-(aq) \rightarrow Na^+Cl^-(aq) + NH_3(g)$

Many different ammonium salts are made from ammonia. These contain different percentages of nitrogen. Different crops need different proportions of N, P, K in fertilisers. You need to be able to calculate these percentages.

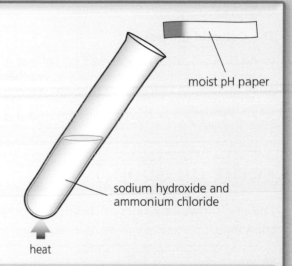

moist pH paper

sodium hydroxide and ammonium chloride

heat

Percentage composition

Ammonium nitrate, NH_4NO_3 is used as a fertiliser but how much nitrogen does it contain?

To work out a percentage composition, first calculate the relative formula mass of the chemical.

Relative formula mass of NH_4NO_3
$= 14 + (4 \times 1) + 14 + (3 \times 16) = 80$

Then calculate the total mass of the element you are asked about. Notice here that there are two nitrogen atoms. $2 \times 14 = 28$

Now turn this into a percentage of the total relative formula mass:

$\% \text{ nitrogen} = \dfrac{\text{Total mass of nitrogen} \times 100}{\text{Relative formula mass (of ammonium nitrate)}} = \dfrac{28 \times 100}{80} = 35$

So ammonium nitrate contains 35% nitrogen.

You can use the same process to calculate the % of potassium in potassium nitrate KNO_3. (39%)

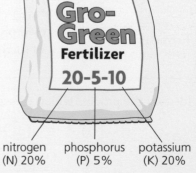

Gro-Green Fertilizer

20-5-10

nitrogen (N) 20% phosphorus (P) 5% potassium (K) 20%

continued

What you should know at Credit level – continued

The Haber Process

The reaction that produces ammonia is a reversible reaction. This means that it goes in both directions.

This can be shown in the following way:

$$N_2 + 3H_2 \rightleftharpoons 2NH_3$$

Some of the nitrogen and hydrogen react to make ammonia but at the same time some of the ammonia breaks down to reform nitrogen and hydrogen. The break down rate of ammonia is increased as the temperature rises. A temperature of 400°C to 500°C is chosen for the Haber process. This is a compromise between a reasonable rate of reaction and a reasonable yield. At lower temperatures there is a better yield but the reaction is too slow to be economic.

The Ostwald process

In the Ostwald process ammonia is passed over a heated platinum catalyst. The oxidation of ammonia is an **exothermic** reaction and produces enough heat to keep the catalyst hot. It is not necessary to continue to supply heat once the reaction has started. The reaction is kept at about 600°C to prevent too much of the ammonia breaking up.

Look out for

Make sure you know which catalyst is used in the Haber and Ostwald processes. You should also know that the platinum catalyst used in the Ostwald process is heated to start the reaction. The heating can be discontinued once the reaction starts. The reaction is exothermic and keeps the catalyst hot.

Credit question 1

The grid shows the names of chemical processes which involve catalysts.

A	B	C
Haber Process	Ostwald Process	Cracking of hydrocarbons
D	E	F
Fermentation	Hydrolysis of sucrose	Formation of alkanes from alkenes

(a) Identify the process which uses ammonia as a **reactant.**

A	B	C
D	E	F

(b) Identify the two processes in which hydrogen is a reactant.

A	B	C
D	E	F

Ammonia is used as a reactant in the Ostwald process. Note that ammonia is the product in the Haber process.

*You should know that **hydrogen** is a reactant in the Haber process (A). This gives you one answer now look at the other processes.*

B uses ammonia, air and water as reactants.

C uses hydrocarbons as reactants.

D uses carbohydrates as reactants

E uses sucrose and water as reactants.

*F Here you will have to work out that **hydrogen** is needed to convert alkenes to alkanes. For example to convert ethene C_2H_4 to ethane C_2H_6 you have to **add** H_2. So here hydrogen is a reactant. (F) is the second answer.*

Credit question 2

The grid shows the formulae of pairs of chemicals.

A NaOH HNO_3	B $Ca(OH)_2$ NH_4NO_3	C NH_3 HCl
D KNO_3 $CuSO_4$	E KNO_3 NH_4NO_3	F N_2 H_2

(a) Identify the **pair** of chemicals which could be heated together to make ammonia in the laboratory.

A	B	C
D	E	F

Look out for

Be prepared for questions about the preparation of ammonia in the laboratory, they turn up regularly. You can heat any alkali and any ammonium salt to produce ammonia. If ammonia is produced when an ammonium salt is heated with an unknown substance you can deduce that the unknown substance is an alkali.

(b) Identify the pair of chemicals where both can be used as fertilisers.

A	B	C
D	E	F

The chemicals are listed in pairs so the question is only looking for **one** answer. Take each pair in turn

A This is an alkali and an acid. They will make a salt and water. ✗

B This is an alkali and an ammonium salt. You need to learn that **any ammonium salt and any alkali will react to produce ammonia**. This can be used in the laboratory to make ammonia. ✓

C This pair will react to make ammonium chloride only. ✗

D These are both salts and will not react. ✗

E These are both nitrates and will not react. ✗

F Although nitrogen and hydrogen react to make ammonia you would not use this in the laboratory. These are used in the industrial process. The pressures you would need are not easily obtained in the lab. ✗

Fertilisers provide **at least one of the N, P, K** nutrients. Take each pair in turn.

A NaOH is not a nutrient provider ✗

B $Ca(OH)_2$ is not a nutrient provider. ✗

C HCl is not a nutrient provider. ✗

D $CuSO_4$ is not a nutrient provider. ✗

E Both of these chemicals are nitrates so will provide nitrogen. In addition the KNO_3 provides potassium. Both can be used as fertilisers. ✓

F Although plants need nitrogen they need **fixed** nitrogen in the form of compounds. Plants cannot use **free** nitrogen, N_2. ✗

Credit question 3

Nitrogen forms many useful compounds.

Compound	Formula	Solubility in water
Y	$(NH_4)_2SO_4$	very
potassium nitrate	KNO_3	very
urea	$CO(NH_2)_2$	slightly

The ammonium ion and the sulphate ion are shown on p4 of the data booklet. Be careful that you do not mix up ammonia with ammonium.

(a) Name compound **Y**.

 Compound Y is ammonium sulphate.

(b) Compound **Y** is mixed with potassium nitrate to make a fertiliser.

 (i) Why are fertilisers added to the soil?

 Fertilisers are added to **restore** the essential elements needed for plant growth. Or Fertilisers are added to **replace** the essential elements removed by cropping plants.

 (ii) Which essential plant nutrient is **not** present in this fertiliser mix?

 It does not contain phosphorous.

There are three essential plant nutrients. Nitrogen (N), phosphorous (P) and potassium (K). This mix **does not** contain any **phosphorous (P)**.

(c) Urea is used as a fertiliser in areas of high rainfall.

 (i) Give a reason why urea is chosen for these areas.

 Urea is not as soluble as other fertilisers. It is less likely to be washed away.

 (ii) Calculate the percentage of nitrogen in urea.

 _It is 47%._

Calculate the relative formula mass of urea,
$CO(NH_2)_2$ 12 + 16 + (2 x 14) + (4 x 1) = 60
then calculate the mass of nitrogen. There are two nitrogen atoms
2 x 14 = 28.
Calculate the percentage of nitrogen:

$$\% \text{ nitrogen} = \frac{\text{Total mass of nitrogen} \times 100}{\text{Relative formula mass (of urea)}} = \frac{28 \times 100}{60} = 46.67\% \text{ or } 47\%$$

Look out for

Try to practice calculations involving the percentage composition of a chemical. Make sure that you count **all** of the atoms of the element whose percentage you have to calculate.

Credit question 4

The flow chart shows some processes which take place in an industrial chemical factory.

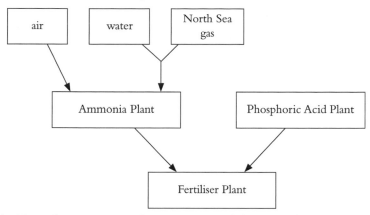

(a) Air and water are used as raw materials because they contain the elements needed to make ammonia.
Suggest **one** other reason why they are used as raw materials.

Air and water are used as raw materials because they are
readily available.

(b) Which reactant for the ammonia plant must be produced in the reaction between North Sea gas and water?

Hydrogen.

(c) Name the salt formed in the fertiliser plant.

*The salt formed will be **ammonium phosphate**.*

You could also say that they do not come from **finite resources** or they are **not expensive**. You should **not** say that they are free because they will have to be processed before they can be used and this costs money.

Ammonia contains nitrogen and hydrogen. The nitrogen can be extracted from the air. Both water and North Sea gas (methane) contain hydrogen. They are used as the source of hydrogen.

Ammonia is reacted with phosphoric acid

(d) The graph shows the different percentage yields of ammonia which can be obtained under different conditions in the ammonia plant.

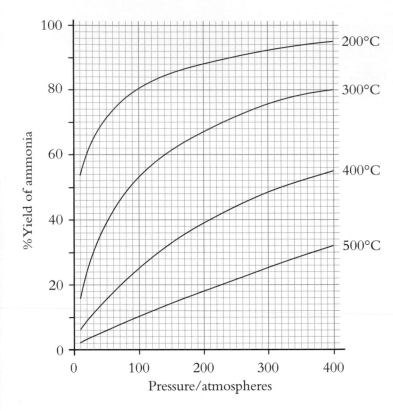

(i) What is the relationship between the percentage yield of ammonia and the temperature at constant pressure?

As the temperature increases the percentage yield decreases.

(ii) Explain why all of the nitrogen and hydrogen are not converted to ammonia.

Some of the ammonia *that is made will break down to* **reform the nitrogen and hydrogen**.

The reaction between nitrogen and hydrogen to make ammonia is a **reversible** reaction.

$$N_2 + 3H_2 \rightleftharpoons 2NH_3$$

*You are **not** being asked to quote a particular yield at a particular temperature and pressure but give the **trend**. It is not good enough to say ' it increases' or 'it decreases'. You need to relate the yield to the temperature. What you need to do here is pick a pressure. Take 200 atmospheres. Now look at the yields at this pressure and at different temperatures. Note that the temperatures here are **decreasing** as you go up the Y-axis.*

At 200°C and 200 atmospheres the yield is 88%. At 300°C the yield is 67%. At 400°C the yield is 39%.

As the temperature increases the percentage yield decreases. *It will not matter which pressure you choose. You will get the same answer.*

Look out for

If you are asked to describe a trend do not give a set of specific readings. You should not describe the graph in detail. Look for the pattern. If you are asked to describe a relationship you have to link two things together.

Carbohydrates and related substances

What you should know at General **level...**

Photosynthesis is the process by which plants make carbohydrates. Plants absorb carbon dioxide from the atmosphere and water from the soil and convert them into glucose and oxygen. Energy is needed for the reaction to take place and it is provided by the Sun. A chemical called chlorophyll is also essential for the process. It is present in the green parts of plants and its role is to absorb the light energy from the Sun.

$$\text{carbon dioxide} \quad + \quad \text{water} \quad \xrightarrow[\text{light energy}]{\text{chlorophyll}} \quad \text{glucose} \quad + \quad \text{oxygen}$$

$$6CO_2 \quad + \quad 6H_2O \quad \rightarrow \quad C_6H_{12}O_6 \quad + \quad 6O_2$$

Photosynthesis is a vital chemical reaction. It produces oxygen and stores the Sun's energy in the form of carbohydrates. Plants and animals use these carbohydrates as an energy source.

Respiration is the process that plants and animals use to get their energy. Glucose is converted into carbon dioxide and water using oxygen thereby releasing the trapped chemical energy.

$$\text{glucose} \quad + \quad \text{oxygen} \quad \rightarrow \quad \text{carbon dioxide} \quad + \quad \text{water}$$

$$C_6H_{12}O_6 \quad + \quad 6O_2 \quad \rightarrow \quad 6CO_2 \quad + \quad 6H_2O$$

Animals use the energy released to keep their bodies warm, move about and keep their heart, brain and other life functions working.

Photosynthesis and respiration are the reverse of one another. Provided they keep in balance we do not need to be worried about having enough food or oxygen.

There is a small percentage of carbon dioxide in the atmosphere. It is important that this does not increase too much as carbon dioxide is a **greenhouse gas**. It traps the Sun's energy and leads to an increase in the temperature of the Earth. This is called **global warming**. Global warming is causing the polar ice caps to shrink, sea levels to rise and unwanted changes to seasonal weather.

The percentage of carbon dioxide in the atmosphere is rising. This is due to the burning of fossil fuels. Moreover, cutting down rain forests removes plants that would be absorbing this additional carbon dioxide.

Carbohydrates

- are compounds containing carbon, hydrogen and oxygen.
- have a formula of the type $C_x(H_2O)_y$.
- include:
  - polymers like starch. Starch is not sweet and does not dissolve in water. A beam of light **does** show up when passed through a suspension of starch in water. (Tyndall beam)
  - sugars such as glucose and sucrose. These dissolve well in water and taste sweet. A beam of light **does not** show up when passed through a sugar solution.

continued

Look out for

Learn the equations for photosynthesis and respiration. Make sure that you can recognise these and the role that they play in keeping carbon dioxide levels in the atmosphere steady. Remember that clearing rain forests does not **increase** carbon dioxide levels but reduces the amount of carbon dioxide that is **removed** from the atmosphere. The major cause of the increase in carbon dioxide levels is the increasing use of fossil fuels.

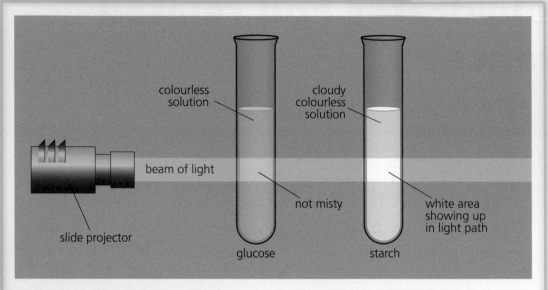

▶ can be classed as
  ▶ monosaccharides like glucose and fructose. They have the fomula $C_6H_{12}O_6$
  ▶ disaccharides like sucrose, lactose and maltose. They have the formula $C_{12}H_{22}O_{11}$
  ▶ polysaccharides like starch. This can be represented by the formula $(C_6H_{10}O_5)_n$ where n represents a very large number.

Tests for carbohydrates include:

▶ **Benedict's test** – Benedict's solution is a clear blue colour. It gives a positive test by turning cloudy orange **when heated** with **glucose**. Benedict's solution **cannot** be used to test for sucrose or starch. **Fehling's** solution gives a similar colour change and can be used instead of Benedict's solution to test for glucose.
▶ **Iodine test** – iodine solution turns blue/black with **starch**.

Starch

▶ is a polymer made up of glucose monomer units. Glucose ($C_6H_{12}O_6$) can be represented as   HO⟨ **G** ⟩OH

We can use these to represent glucose molecules joining to form part of a starch molecule. This is called a polymerisation reaction. The glucose molecules join up to make one larger starch molecule.

HO⟨ **G** ⟩O H + HO⟨ **G** ⟩O H + HO⟨ **G** ⟩OH   3 glucose molecules

↓

−O⟨ **G** ⟩O⟨ **G** ⟩O⟨ **G** ⟩O−   part of a starch molecule containing 3 glucose molecules joined together

+ H_2O + H_2O

or we can represent this reaction by the equations

n(glucose) → starch + water

$n(C_6H_{12}O_6)$ → $(C_6H_{10}O_5)_n$ + nH_2O

continued

What you should know at General level – continued

- is a large molecule and cannot pass through the gut wall.
- can be broken down into small glucose molecules which can pass through the gut wall. This happens during digestion. Acids or enzymes catalyse the break down of starch. **Enzymes** are biological catalysts.

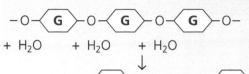

part of a starch molecule containing 3 glucose molecules joined together

3 glucose molecules

The breakdown of starch can be represented by the equations:

$$starch \quad + \quad water \quad \rightarrow \quad glucose$$
$$(C_6H_{10}O_5)_n \quad + \quad nH_2O \quad \rightarrow \quad n(C_6H_{12}O_6)$$

This breakdown can also be carried out in the laboratory by heating starch with a dilute acid. You can show that the starch has been broken down by testing before and after with Benedict's solution. There is no reaction before heating but there is a positive reaction after. It is also possible to use enzymes in the laboratory. Starch can be **warmed** with a solution of amylase, this will cause the starch to break down into glucose.

Alcohol

- is a member of the alkanol family and is called **ethanol**. Ethanol has the chemical formula C_2H_5OH and the structural formula:
- can be made from any fruit or vegetable, which is a source of sugar or starch, by a process called **fermentation**.
- is found in alcoholic drinks like wine made from grapes and beer made from barley.
- is produced when the enzymes present in yeast convert glucose into ethanol and carbon dioxide. The equation for this reaction is:

$$glucose \quad \rightarrow \quad ethanol \quad + \quad carbon\ dioxide$$
$$C_6H_{12}O_6 \quad \rightarrow \quad 2C_2H_5OH \quad + \quad 2CO_2$$

The concentration of alcohol produced by fermentation is limited to about 15%. Higher concentrations of alcohol can be produced by **distillation**. Alcohol (ethanol) has a lower boiling point than water so boils before water. The separation of ethanol and water by distillation depends on this difference in boiling point. Alcoholic drinks like whisky and brandy are produced by fermentation followed by distillation.

Look out for

Notice that the formation of starch from glucose and the breakdown of starch to form glucose are the reverse of one another.

15

General question 1

The grid shows the names of some gases.

A methane	B nitrogen	C carbon monoxide
D oxygen	E carbon dioxide	F nitrogen dioxide

Identify the gas produced by respiration and combustion.

A	B	C
D	(E)	F

Carbon monoxide can be produced by combustion but is not produced during respiration. Carbon dioxide is the only gas which answers this question.

General question 2

The grid shows the names of chemical processes or chemical reactions.

A respiration	B fermentation	C filtration
D condensation	E distillation	F photosynthesis

(a) Identify the process which is used to separate alcohol from water.

A	B	C
(D)	E	F

*Alcohol is **produced** by fermentation but this will only produce about 15% alcohol. The alcohol can be separated from water by **distillation**, because alcohol and water have different boiling points.*

(b) Identify the process in which chlorophyll absorbs light energy.

A	B	C
D	E	(F)

(c) Identify the **two** processes in which carbon dioxide is released.

(A)	(B)	C
D	E	F

You cannot work this out from the question. You have to know that carbon dioxide is released by respiration and fermentation.

Look out for

Make sure you know what is meant by fermentation and distillation.

General question 3

The flow chart shows the main stages in making malt vinegar.

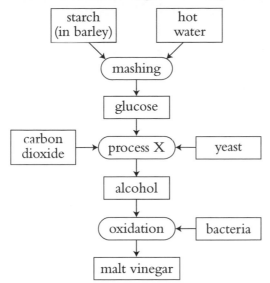

(a) In the mashing process some of the starch is broken down into glucose. Starch and glucose are carbohydrates. Name the elements present in carbohydrates.

Carbon, hydrogen and oxygen.

(b) Describe how you could test the mash to see if it still contained some starch.

Add iodine solution to a sample of the mash. If starch is present it would turn blue/black.

(c) What name is given to process X?

*It is called **fermentation.***

You should know that carbohydrates contain carbon, hydrogen and oxygen. There is a clue in the name as it ends in 'ate' so is likely to contain three elements of which one is oxygen. Carbohydrates have a formula of the type $C_x(H_2O)_y$.

Do not be put off by the unfamiliar setting of this question. Remember that you have to give both the reagent and the result if you are asked for a test.

Look at the flow chart. Yeast is being added to glucose to make alcohol – fermentation.

General question 4

Starch and glucose are carbohydrates.

(a) Which solution do you use to test for glucose and what colour change will you see?

Benedict's *solution will change from **blue** to **orange** when heated with glucose.*

*__Benedict's__ solution will change colour from (clear) **blue** to (cloudy) **orange** (when heated) with glucose. You do not need to include the words in brackets but you must give the colour change.*

Look out for

Learn the tests for starch and glucose. You need to know the names of the test solutions and the conditions. You have to **heat** Benedict's solution but **not** heat iodine solution. Remember when you use a test solution you should also give the colour for a positive test. If you are asked about a colour change you must give the colour before and after. It is a good idea to write out a list of all the chemical tests you have met in Standard Grade. Make a list of the chemicals or names and the results of a positive test.

(b) What is the chemical name for the alcohol produced by the fermentation of glucose?

The alcohol is called **ethanol**.

(c) The percentage of alcohol in a wine depends on the temperature of the fermentation process. Some results are shown on the graph.

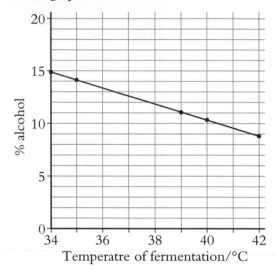

Temperatre of fermentation/°C

Here you are being asked to describe the **general** trend in the graph not what is happening at any particular temperature. You need to relate temperature and %. It is not good enough to say 'it goes down' as you have not said what 'it' is.

(i) Describe how the temperature of fermentation affects the % of alcohol produced.

As the temperature increases the % of alcohol goes down.

(ii) Use the graph to estimate the % of alcohol when the temperature is 37 °C.

The answer is **12½%**.

Look at the scale for temperature on the **x**-axis, 37 is not marked but you should see that it would be on a line between 36 and 38. Follow this line up until it meets the line of the graph. Check the scale on the **y**-axis. Each square represents 1%. You should get the answer 12½% but any answer between 12% and 13% will be acceptable.

What you should know at **Credit** level...

When you burn a carbohydrate in a plentiful supply of air it produces carbon dioxide and water. This shows that carbohydrates contain carbon and hydrogen. It does not show that carbohydrates contain oxygen because most of the oxygen present in the carbon dioxide and water products comes from the air.

Glucose and fructose are **isomers**. They have the same chemical formula but different structures.

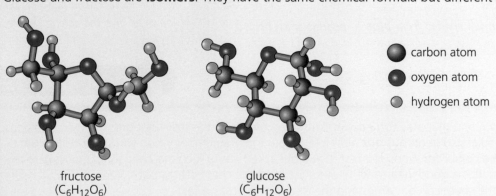

- carbon atom
- oxygen atom
- hydrogen atom

fructose
($C_6H_{12}O_6$)

glucose
($C_6H_{12}O_6$)

continued

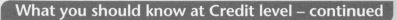
What you should know at Credit level – continued

Sucrose and maltose are also isomers.

Benedict's or Fehling's reagent can be used to test for **reducing** sugars like glucose, fructose and maltose. Sucrose is **not** a reducing sugar so does not react with these reagents.

The joining of glucose molecules to form starch is an example of **condensation polymerisation**.

The glucose molecules link up by losing water.

$$n(\text{glucose}) \rightarrow \text{starch} + \text{water}$$
$$n(C_6H_{12}O_6) \rightarrow (C_6H_{10}O_5)_n + nH_2O$$
$$\text{monosaccharide} \qquad \text{polysaccharide}$$

The **reverse** of this reaction is the breakdown of starch into glucose by the addition of water. This is called **hydrolysis**. This process happens during digestion. The presence of acids and/or enzymes speed up hydrolysis.

$$\text{starch} + \text{water} \rightarrow n(\text{glucose})$$
$$(C_6H_{10}O_5)_n + nH_2O \rightarrow n(C_6H_{12}O_6)$$
$$\text{polysaccharide} \qquad \text{monosaccharide}$$

Disaccharides like sucrose also undergo **hydrolysis** in the presence of acid and/or enzymes. Disaccharides are broken down into monosaccharides by reaction with water.

$$C_{12}H_{22}O_{11} + H_2O \rightarrow C_6H_{12}O_6 + C_6H_{12}O_6$$
$$\text{disaccharide} + \text{water} \rightarrow \text{monosaccharide} + \text{monosaccharide}$$

This reaction is one of the reactions which occur in the human body during digestion. Human enzymes work best at a temperature of 37°C, body temperature. Enzymes are denatured (destroyed) by high temperatures and also by very acidic or alkaline conditions.

Credit question 1

Carbohydrates are formed in plants.

A		B		C	
	starch		glucose		maltose
D		E			
	sucrose		fructose		

(a) Identify the carbohydrate which does not dissolve well in water.

Ⓐ	B	C
D	E	

*You should know that sugars are soluble in water but **starch** is not soluble. Starch forms a colloidal suspension in water. If you shine a light through this suspension you can see the path of the light. This does not happen with a solution of sugars.*

(b) Identify the two carbohydrates with the formula $C_{12}H_{22}O_{11}$.

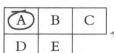

A	B	Ⓒ
Ⓓ	E	

*Carbohydrates with twelve carbon atoms in each molecule are called disaccharides. You cannot guess at the names and should learn that **maltose** and **sucrose** are disaccharides.*

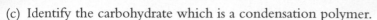

(c) Identify the carbohydrate which is a condensation polymer.

Ⓐ	B	C
D	E	

(d) Identify the two carbohydrates which cannot be hydrolysed.

A	Ⓑ	C
D	Ⓔ	

*Carbohydrates which cannot be hydrolysed are monosaccharides. They cannot be broken down into smaller carbohydrates. The answers are **glucose** and **fructose**. Again it is wise to learn the names of the monosaccharides you have met in this topic.*

Credit question 2

There are different types of chemical reaction

A		B		C	
respiration		fermentation		hydrolysis	
D		E		F	
condensation		redox		photosynthesis	

(a) Identify the reaction in which glucose is converted to starch.

A	B	C
Ⓓ	E	F

*Glucose is a monosaccharide and joins together to from the polysaccharide starch in a process called condensation polymerisation. The answer you are looking for here is **condensation**.*

Look out for

Make sure you understand condensation reactions. Small molecules join together by losing water. For example two glucose molecules can join together to make maltose.

$$C_6H_{12}O_6 + C_6H_{12}O_6 \rightarrow C_{12}H_{22}O_{11} + H_2O$$

glucose + glucose → maltose + water

This is an example of **condensation** but not polymerisation. Maltose is a disaccharide **not** a polymer. Starch is made from the **condensation polymerisation** of glucose.

(b) Identify the reaction

$$(C_6H_{10}O_5)_n + nH_2O \rightarrow n(C_6H_{12}O_6)$$

A	B	Ⓒ
D	E	F

*This equation represents the conversion of starch to glucose. It shows a large molecule being broken down into smaller molecules by the addition of water. This is an example of **hydrolysis**.*

Credit question 3

Fermentation is used to produce alcohol from sugars like glucose.

(a) Name the gas produced during fermentation.

   The gas produced during fermentation is **carbon dioxide**.

You can either write the name or the formula CO_2.

(b) Why does fermentation stop when the alcohol concentration reaches approximately 15%?

   The **enzymes** *are* **denatured** *by high concentrations of alcohol and can no longer catalyse the reactions.*

Yeast is needed for fermentation. It is the enzymes in yeast that catalyse the reactions which produce alcohol.

(c) In industry ethanol (alcohol) is made from ethene as shown below.

$$H-\underset{\underset{H}{|}}{\overset{\overset{H}{|}}{C}}=\underset{\underset{H}{|}}{\overset{\overset{H}{|}}{C}}-H \quad + \quad H_2O \quad \rightarrow \quad H-\underset{\underset{H}{|}}{\overset{\overset{H}{|}}{C}}-\underset{\underset{H}{|}}{\overset{\overset{OH}{|}}{C}}-H$$

   ethene   ethanol

   (i) Name the type of chemical reaction taking place.

   This is an example of an **addition** *reaction.*

   (ii) Draw the structural formula for the product of the following reaction

$$H-\underset{\underset{H}{|}}{\overset{\overset{H}{|}}{C}}=\underset{\underset{CH_3}{|}}{\overset{\overset{H}{|}}{C}}-\underset{\underset{H}{|}}{\overset{\overset{H}{|}}{C}}-\underset{\underset{H}{|}}{\overset{\overset{H}{|}}{C}}-H \quad + \quad H_2O \quad \longrightarrow \quad H-\underset{\underset{H}{|}}{\overset{\overset{OH}{|}}{C}}-\underset{\underset{CH_3}{|}}{\overset{\overset{H}{|}}{C}}-\underset{\underset{H}{|}}{\overset{\overset{H}{|}}{C}}-\underset{\underset{H}{|}}{\overset{\overset{H}{|}}{C}}-H$$

Look out for

Be aware of the effect of high alcohol concentration and high temperature in denaturing enzymes. Remember enzymes are not living organisms so cannot be killed but are **denatured**.

Ethene contains a double bond and the water adds across this bond.

Look at the example above in (i). You have to add H_2O to the structure drawn in the question. Remember that in an addition reaction the product will no longer have a double bond. Watch also that you include the CH_3 group on the second carbon atom. You could also show the OH on same C as the CH_3. Either formula will be accepted.

Credit question 4

Ailsa carried out the experiment shown below.

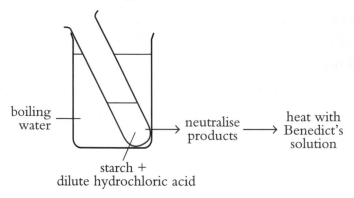

boiling water

starch + dilute hydrochloric acid

→ neutralise products → heat with Benedict's solution

Result: Benedict's solution turns red/orange

(a) (i) What type of chemical reaction takes place when starch is heated with dilute hydrochloric acid?

   A **hydrolysis** reaction is taking place.

Remember that starch does not react with Benedict's solution, but after heating with acid the products of the reaction do react with Benedict's solution. Starch which is a polysaccharide, has been broken down into monosaccharides. This is an example of **hydrolysis**. The acid acts as a catalyst.

(ii) Ailsa said that the starch had been turned into glucose. Name another sugar which turns Benedict's solution red/orange.

   Fructose.

Here you have a choice of answers. Any of **fructose, maltose or lactose**. Remember that you **cannot** use **sucrose** as it does not react with Benedict's solution.

(iii) Ailsa repeated her experiment using amylase solution instead of hydrochloric acid.
   Suggest a reason why the Benedict's solution did not turn red/orange.

   The enzyme **amylase** would have been denatured and the
   hydrolysis reaction would not have taken place and no
   monosaccharide would be formed.

(b) Write the molecular formula for glucose.

   Glucose has the formula $C_6H_{12}O_6$.

You really need to study the diagram here. Ailsa would have placed the starch and amylase mixture in a water bath of boiling water. Amylase is an enzyme and is **denatured** by high temperatures. The denatured enzyme cannot catalyse the hydrolysis of starch so there will be no colour change with Benedict's solution.

Chemical tests

Acids	turn pH paper or universal indicator solution red.
Alkalis	turn pH paper or universal indicator solution blue/purple.
Carbon dioxide	turns lime water milky.
Glucose (or fructose or maltose)	turns warm blue Benedict's solution (or Fehling's solution) cloudy orange.
Hydrogen	burns with a squeaky pop on applying a lighted splint.
Hydroxide ions (OH⁻(aq))	turn yellow ferroxyl indicator pink.
Iron(II) ions (Fe²⁺(aq))	turn yellow ferroxyl indicator blue.
Oxygen	relights a glowing splint.
Starch	turns brown iodine solution blue/black.
Unsaturated hydrocarbons	turn orange/red bromine solution colourless.
Water	turns blue cobalt chloride paper pink.

Glossary

Acid   A substance that forms a solution with a pH less than 7.

Acidic solution   A solution which contains an excess of hydrogen ions ($H^+(aq)$).

Acid rain   Rain containing dissolved sulphur dioxide and/ or nitrogen dioxide. It has damaging effects on buildings, structures made of iron or steel, soils, and plant and animal life.

Addition   The reaction that takes place when a molecule such as hydrogen or bromine 'adds on' across the carbon-to-carbon double bond in an alkene.

Addition polymer   A large molecule that is formed when unsaturated monomer units join together. Examples include poly(propene) which is formed from propene monomer units.

Addition polymerisation   The reaction that takes place when unsaturated monomers link up through their carbon-to-carbon double bonds to form large polymer molecules.

Air   A mixture of gases – approximately 80% nitrogen and 20% oxygen.

Alkali   A substance that forms a solution with a pH greater than 7.

Alkali metals   The family of reactive metals in Group 1 of the Periodic Table.

Alkaline solution   A solution which contains an excess of hydroxide ions ($OH^-(aq)$).

Alkanes   A family of saturated hydrocarbons which have the general formula C_nH_{2n+2}.

Alkenes   A family of unsaturated hydrocarbons which have the general formula C_nH_{2n}. They all contain a carbon-to-carbon double bond.

Alloy   A mixture of metals or a mixture of metals and non-metals. Brass, solder and steel are examples of alloys.

Amylase   The enzyme present in saliva which catalyses the hydrolysis of starch.

Atomic number   The number of protons in an atom of an element.

Atoms   The tiny particles that make up elements. An atom consists of a positively charged nucleus with negatively charged electrons moving around outside the nucleus. It has no overall charge.

Base   A substance which neutralises an acid. Examples include metal oxides, metal hydroxides, metal carbonates and ammonia. Those bases which are soluble in water form alkalis.

Battery   A collection of two or more cells joined together.

Biodegradable   Able to be broken down by bacteria in the soil and eventually rot away.

Blast furnace   A furnace in which iron is extracted from its ore (Fe_2O_3).

Burning   A chemical reaction in which a substance reacts with oxygen in the air and produces heat energy.

Carbohydrates   Compounds containing carbon, hydrogen and oxygen in which the ratio of hydrogen to oxygen is 2:1. They are used by the body to produce energy.

Carbon monoxide   A poisonous gas formed when carbon-containing compounds burn in a limited supply of air.

Catalyst   A substance which speeds up a chemical reaction. By the end of the reaction a catalyst is unchanged chemically and the same mass is present as there was at the start.

Catalytic converters   A device which is fitted to exhausts to speed up the conversion of pollutant gases into less harmful gases.

Cell   A device which produces electricity from a chemical reaction. Chemical energy is converted into electrical energy.

Chemical formula   A shorthand way of representing a substance. It shows what elements are present in the substance and the number of atoms of each e.g. CO_2 is the formula for carbon dioxide and shows that one molecule of carbon dioxide contains one carbon atom and two oxygen atoms.

Chemical reaction   A process in which substances change to form one or more new substances.

Chemical symbol   A shorthand way of representing an element. It consists of one or two letters e.g. C for carbon and Co for cobalt.

Chlorophyll   A green-coloured compound present in the green parts of plants. It absorbs light energy needed for photosynthesis.

Coal   A solid fossil fuel which is mainly carbon.

Combustion   Another word for burning.

Complete combustion   When a substance burns completely in a plentiful supply of air.

Compound   A substance in which two or more elements are chemically joined.

Condensation   A reaction in which two small molecules join together to form a larger molecule. A water molecule is released in the process.

Condensation polymer   A large molecule that is formed when monomer units join together with the release of water. Examples include starch which is formed from glucose monomer units.

Condensation polymerisation   The reaction that takes place when monomers join up to form large polymer molecules with the release of water.

Corrosion   A chemical reaction that takes place on the surface of a metal. The metal reacts with substances in the air to form a compound. Iron rusting is an example of corrosion.

Covalent bond   A covalent bond is formed when two atoms of (usually) non-metal elements share a pair of electrons. It is the force of attraction between the negatively charged shared pair of electrons and the positively charged nuclei on either side that hold the atoms together.

Covalent molecular substances   Substances made up of small separate molecules with strong covalent bonds **inside** the molecules and weak bonds **between** the molecules. They have low melting and boiling points and do not conduct electricity in any state. Examples include bromine (Br_2) and ammonia (NH_3).

Covalent network substances   Substances made up of giant molecules in which the atoms are joined by strong covalent bonds. They have high melting and boiling points and do not conduct electricity in any state. Examples include diamond (C) and silicon dioxide (SiO_2).

Cracking   A chemical reaction in which large hydrocarbons are broken down into a mixture of smaller, more useful hydrocarbons. Some of the smaller hydrocarbons produced are unsaturated.

Crude oil   A liquid fossil fuel which contains a mixture of hydrocarbons.

Cycloalkanes   A family of saturated hydrocarbons which have the general formula C_nH_{2n}. They all contain a ring of carbon atoms.

Diatomic molecule   A molecule which contains only two atoms, e.g. H_2 and CO.

Digestion   The breaking down of large food molecules into smaller ones so that they can pass through the gut wall into the blood stream. For example, starch is digested into glucose.

Dilute solution   A solution in which a small amount of substance (solute) has been dissolved.

Disaccharides   Simple carbohydrate molecules with the molecular formula $C_{12}H_{22}O_{11}$. They are formed when two monosaccharides condense together. Examples include sucrose and maltose.

Displacement   A reaction that takes place when a metal is added to a solution containing ions of a metal lower in the electrochemical series or when a metal reacts with an acid.

Distillation   A method of separating liquids which have different boiling points. It is used to increase the alcohol concentration of fermented mixtures.

Electric current   A flow of charged particles. Electrons flow through metals. Ions flow through solutions and melts of ionic compounds.

Electrical conductor   A substance which allows a current of electricity to pass through it.

Electrical insulator   A substance which does not allow a current of electricity to pass through it.

Electrochemical series   A list of metals (and hydrogen) arranged in order of their ability to form ions in solution. An electrochemical series can be found on page 7 of your data booklet.

Electrolysis   A process in which a current of electricity is passed through an electrolyte resulting in the breakup of the electrolyte. For example, when copper chloride solution is electrolysed it breaks up to form copper and chlorine.

Electron   A tiny particle in an atom which is located outside the nucleus. It has a very small mass and a charge of 1−.

Electron arrangement   The arrangement of electrons in shells (or energy levels) around the nucleus of an atom. The electron arrangements of some elements can be found on page 1 of your data booklet.

Electroplating   A process in which a thin layer of a metal is coated on to another metal by electrolysis. Iron can be electroplated with another metal in order to prevent it rusting.

Element   A substance which cannot be broken down into a simpler substance. All the elements are listed in the Periodic Table on page 8 of your Data Booklet.

Empirical formula   The formula of a compound which shows the simplest whole number ratio of the different atoms in the compound.

Enzyme   A catalyst which speeds up chemical reactions in living things, i.e. a biological catalyst

Essential elements   These are nitrogen (N), phosphorus (P) and potassium (K) and are needed for healthy plant growth.

Ethanol   The alcohol present in alcoholic drinks. It can be made by the fermentation of carbohydrates.

Exothermic reaction   A reaction in which energy is released.

Fermentation   A chemical reaction in which glucose is broken down into alcohol (ethanol) and carbon dioxide. It is catalysed by enzymes present in yeast.

Fertiliser   A natural or artificial substance which is added to the soil to restore essential nutrients.

Fibres   Thin thread-like strands used to make clothing fabrics. They are made up of long chain molecules called polymers.

Finite resource   A limited amount of a resource. Examples include the fossil fuels.

Fixed nitrogen   Nitrogen which is present in a compound and chemically joined with other elements.

Flammability   A measure of how easily a substance catches fire.

Formula equation   A shorthand way of describing a chemical reaction showing the formulae of the reactants and products, e.g. $Mg(s) + 2HCl(aq) \rightarrow H_2(g) + MgCl_2(aq)$

Fossil fuels   They are coal, oil, natural gas and were formed over millions of years from the remains of dead animals and plants.

Fraction   A mixture of hydrocarbons with boiling points within a certain range of temperature.

Fractional distillation   The process used to separate crude oil into fractions according to the different boiling points of the hydrocarbons in crude oil.

Free nitrogen   Nitrogen which is not combined with another element but simply the element on its own, i.e. $N_2(g)$.

Fuel   A substance which reacts with oxygen (burns) to produce heat energy.

Fuel crisis   A problem caused by not having enough fuel supplies to meet demand.

Galvanising   A process in which iron is coated with zinc in order to prevent rusting.

Global warming   Increasing amounts of carbon dioxide in the atmosphere has caused more of the Sun's energy to be absorbed and has increased the temperature of the atmosphere.

Gram Formula Mass   The mass in grams of one mole of a substance.

Greenhouse effect   This is caused by carbon dioxide in the atmosphere which absorbs some of the Sun's energy and keeps the Earth warm.

Group   A vertical column of elements in the Periodic Table. Elements present in each group have similar chemical properties because their atoms have the same number of outer electrons.

Haber process   The industrial manufacture of ammonia from nitrogen and hydrogen ($N_2 + H_2 \rightarrow NH_3$). The reaction is catalysed by iron.

Halogens   The family of reactive non-metal elements in Group 7 of the Periodic Table.

Homologous series   A family of carbon-containing compounds with similar chemical properties and with the same general formula. Examples include alkanes, alkenes and cycloalkanes.

Hydrocarbon   A compound which contains **only** hydrogen and carbon.

Hydrolysis When a molecule reacts with water and breaks down into smaller molecules. Examples include the breakdown of starch into glucose and the breakdown of sucrose into glucose and fructose.

Incomplete combustion When a substance burns in a limited supply of air.

Insoluble When a substance (solute) does not dissolve in a liquid (solvent), it is said to be insoluble.

Ion-bridge cell A cell in which two half-cells are linked externally by a piece of wire and internally by an ion-bridge. A half-cell consists of a piece of metal dipping into a solution containing ions of that metal. An ion-bridge can be a piece of filter paper soaked in an electrolyte.

Ionic compounds Compounds made up of oppositely charged ions. They have high melting and boiling points because the bonds between ions are very strong and they conduct electricity when dissolved in water and when molten. They usually contain a metal combined with a non-metal.

Ions Tiny particles that are formed when atoms gain or lose electrons. Metal ions have a positive charge while non-metal ions have a negative charge.

Isomers Compounds with the same molecular formula but different structural formulae.

Isotopes Atoms with the same atomic number but different mass numbers or atoms with the same number of protons but different numbers of neutrons

Malleable Can be beaten into different shapes. Metals are malleable.

Mass number The number of protons plus the number of neutrons in an atom of an element.

Metal A type of element. Metals lie to the left of the heavy black line on the Periodic Table on page 8 of your data booklet.

Metal reactivity A measure of how fast a metal reacts with other substances.

Mixture Two or more substances just mixed together but not chemically joined.

Molecule A group of two or more atoms which are held together by strong covalent bonds. A molecule has no overall charge.

Monomer Small molecules that join together to form a large polymer molecule.

Monosaccharides They are the simplest carbohydrates and have the molecular formula $C_6H_{12}O_6$. Examples include glucose and fructose.

Natural fibres Fibres that come from plants and animals. They contain polymer molecules and examples include silk, wool and cotton.

Natural gas A fossil fuel which consists mainly of methane.

Neutral solution A solution with a pH = 7.

Neutraliser A substance which reacts with an acid to form water and cancels out the effect of the acid. Examples include alkalis, metal oxides and metal carbonates.

Neutralisation A chemical reaction which takes place when acids react with neutralisers. Water and a salt are always formed in a neutralisation reaction.

Neutron A tiny particle which is located inside the nucleus of an atom. It has a relative mass of 1 and no charge.

Nitrogen dioxide A poisonous gas formed when nitrogen and oxygen in the air react during lightning storms and around the spark in petrol engines. It causes acid rain.

Noble gases The family of unreactive non-metal elements in Group 0 of the Periodic Table.

Non-metal A type of element. Non-metals lie to the right of the heavy black line on the Periodic Table on page 8 of your data booklet.

Nutrients Substances that are required by growing plants. They include compounds of nitrogen, phosphorus and potassium.

Ores Naturally-occurring compounds of metals.

Ostwald process The industrial manufacture of nitric acid from ammonia. Platinum is used as a catalyst.

Periodic Table An arrangement of the elements in order of increasing atomic number.

pH A number that indicates how acidic or alkaline a solution is.

pH scale A scale which runs from below 0 to above 14 and is a measure of how acidic or alkaline a solution is. Acids have a pH below 7, alkalis have a pH above 7 and neutral solutions have a pH equal to 7.

Photosynthesis A process which takes place in the leaves of plants and involves the conversion of carbon dioxide and water into glucose and oxygen. Light energy and chlorophyll are also required. Photosynthesis is the reverse of respiration.

Physical protection A method of protecting iron from rusting. It consists of placing a surface barrier (paint, grease, plastic, zinc, tin and so on) on the iron which prevents oxygen and water reaching the iron.

Plastics Synthetic materials made up of polymers.

Pollutant Any substance which damages the environment and harms living organisms within the environment.

Polysaccharides They are carbohydrates made up of large polymer molecules with the molecular formula $(C_6H_{10}O_5)_n$. Examples include starch and cellulose.

Polymer A very large molecule which is formed when hundreds of small monomer molecules join together.

Polymerisation A chemical reaction in which small monomer molecules are converted into a large polymer molecule.

Precipitate An insoluble solid that is formed in a precipitation reaction.

Precipitation A reaction which takes place when two solutions are added together and an insoluble product, i.e. a precipitate, is formed.

Proton A tiny particle which is located in the nucleus of an atom. It has a relative mass of 1 and a charge of 1+.

Reaction speed How fast a chemical reaction takes place. It can be affected by changes in particle size, temperature, concentration and the use of a catalyst.

Reactivity series A list of metals arranged in order of reactivity. No reactivity series is shown in your data booklet but the electrochemical series on page 7 is very similar and can be taken as a good guide of metal reactivity.

Redox A reaction in which both reduction and oxidation take place.

Relative atomic mass The average mass of an atom of an element. The relative atomic masses of some elements can be found on page 4 of your data booklet.

Respiration A process whereby all living things get energy from glucose. It involves the reaction between glucose and oxygen to form carbon dioxide and water. Respiration is the reverse of photosynthesis.

Root nodules   Lumps on the roots of plants, such as peas, beans and clover, containing bacteria which convert nitrogen from the air (free nitrogen) into nitrates (fixed nitrogen).

Rusting   The corrosion of iron. Both oxygen and water must be present for iron to rust.

Sacrificial protection   A method of protecting iron from rusting. It involves attaching a metal higher in the electrochemical series to the iron. This metal supplies electrons to the iron and stops rusting.

Salt   A compound in which the hydrogen ions of an acid have been replaced by metal ions or ammonium ions.

Saturated hydrocarbon   A hydrocarbon which contains only single carbon-to-carbon bonds. Examples include the alkanes and cycloalkanes.

Signs of chemical reaction   These include a colour change, a precipitate forming, a gas being given off and a temperature change.

Simple cell   A cell consisting of two different metals (connected by a piece of wire) dipping into an electrolyte.

Soluble   When a substance (solute) dissolves in a liquid (solvent), it is said to be soluble.

Solute   A substance which dissolves in a liquid (solvent) to form a solution.

Solution   A mixture formed when a substance (solute) dissolves in a liquid (solvent).

Solvent   A liquid in which a substance (solute) dissolves.

Spectator ions   Ions which don't take part in a chemical reaction.

Starch   A polymer carbohydrate made in plants from glucose monomer units. It does not readily dissolve in water and is not sweet. It is used as an energy store in plants.

Sugars   Small carbohydrate molecules which are soluble in water and sweet in taste. Examples include glucose, fructose, maltose and sucrose.

Sulphur dioxide   A poisonous gas formed when fossil fuels are burned and it causes acid rain.

Synthetic fibres   Fibres that are manufactured by the chemical industry from crude oil. They are made up of polymer molecules.

Thermoplastic plastic   A plastic that softens on heating and can be reshaped.

Thermosetting plastic   A plastic which does not soften on heating and cannot be reshaped.

Tin-plating iron   A process in which iron is coated with tin in order to prevent corrosion.

Titration   An experimental technique used to determine the concentration of a solution by reacting it with a solution of known concentration.

Toxic   Poisonous

Transition metals   The family of metals which lie between Groups 2 and 3 of the Periodic Table.

Unsaturated hydrocarbon   A hydrocarbon which contains at least one carbon-to-carbon double bond. Examples include the alkenes.

Viscosity   A measure of the thickness of a liquid.

Word equation   A way of describing a chemical reaction showing the names of the reactants and products e.g. sulphur + oxygen → sulphur dioxide.